We've Already Been There

On Feminism and Its Opponents

by
Dr. Gizi Rapaport

Dr. Gizi Rapaport

We've Already Been There
On Feminism and Its Opponents

Senior Editors & Producers: Contento de Semrik

Translator: David Wesley
Editor: Sybil Kaplan
Design: Liliya Lev Ari

ISBN: 978-197-465-945-6

International sole distributor:
Contento de Semrik
22 Isserles Street, 67014, Tel Aviv, Israel
www.Semrik.com
Semrik10@gmail.com

We've Already Been There
On Feminism and Its Opponents

by

Dr. Gizi Rapaport

Contento de Semrik

What can and should a woman be? This is the essential philosophical question at the heart of this book.

Feminist literature dealing with women in modern society focuses for the most part on that which disturbs and rankles; it discusses the trees without relating to the forest. This book attempts to fill that gap; it cuts through to the first principles, laying conceptual foundations for the demand to eliminate the traditional division of roles between the sexes, freeing women from the onus of absolute altruistic morality, which may result in emptiness, boredom, frustration, and even emotional collapse.

However, this book is directed at a male audience no less than at females, raising questions which necessitate male consideration as well as a willingness to change fundamental perceptions. Men may also profit from the past experiences of women; the fate of women throughout history has lessons for men as well — hence the title of this book, with its implicit admonition: *We've Already Been There.*

Dr. Gizi Rapaport taught philosophy of the social sciences and political philosophy at Tel Aviv University. Her Hebrew publications include: *Freedom or Equality?* (1992; published in English in 2012), *On Feminism and its Opponents* (1993), *Beyond Limits: Women vs. Women* (1999); *For a Particular Secular Option: From Monotheism to Rationality* (2005); and *The Best of All Possible Worlds: Confronting the Challenges of Relativism* (2011).

Table of Contents:

3. Woman and the Other

4. The Political Solution

1. Introduction

The modern feminist movement has undergone two phases. In the first phase, the feminist problem was defined and solutions were proposed. The second phase included an attempt to meet the demands of the woman's dual role.

The problem, as determined by the first feminists, was that women were denied the right to act within the wider society and were restricted to household and family roles. These feminists demanded the recognition of equal rights for women, and by extension, demanded access to all opportunities. Betty Friedan, the initiator of the feminist movement in the United States during the 1960s, defined feminism as another stage in the struggle for human rights. Its objective was to bring a majority group into the mainstream of human society. According to Friedan, feminism was as justified as the demand to abolish slavery.

Influenced by the feminist movement, more and more women began to pursue higher education and professional training and to work outside the home.[1] For most women, going out to work meant the expanding of horizons beyond the confines of the home and family. The social interaction and financial reward afforded women independence and the ability to determine their own futures, and it expanded their knowledge and range of interests.[2]

It quickly became apparent that this new freedom had its price. Along with the advantages that accrued from their integration at work, women were now confronted with serious difficulties: in addition to their new undertakings, women also continued to fulfill their traditional roles. The feminist movement was criticized for the fact that all its achievements only meant that now women were expected to work both at home and elsewhere, with 74-85% of all family obligations falling on their shoulders.[3]

This was due to the fact that in most families, in which the woman held a full-time job outside the home, the couple disagreed as to how to divide the household tasks. Many men continued to think that the "woman should continue her obligations as a woman – to rear children and to do the things expected of a woman around the home."[4]

Sylvia Ann Hewlett, author of *A Lesser Life*, notes that the double burden of outside work and work in the home has prevented women from devoting themselves to their work and transforming their jobs into careers. This has resulted in the concentration of women in low-paying jobs.[5]

In its second stage, the feminist movement tried to deal with the problems that the woman's dual role had created. A small number of feminists, who lost hope of changing male patterns of thinking, adopted a radical approach with the aim of enabling women to develop personally and professionally. They rejected the institution of marriage, avoided relations with men, forewent bringing children into the world, and called for the establishment of separate societies for women and men.[6]

According to them, if a woman had to sacrifice her humanity to maintain a relationship with a man, then she had to separate herself from the man who demanded such sacrifice. In contrast, other feminists, such as Betty Friedan (who died in 2006), argued that women should not dissociate themselves from men or deny themselves human or sexual ties with them, and they should not forgo bearing and raising children, because to do so would, in effect, negate the possibility of any human future.[7] She later admitted that she had no unequivocal answer to the question of how a woman who combines career and family should conduct her life. Clearly, Friedan claimed, women should not get stuck at the stage of reacting, and it would be best if the solution were found in cooperation with men. Friedan recognized that there was still a long way to go to achieve feminist objectives, because the social and political climate was largely hostile to the complete and unreserved integration of women in all spheres of activity.[8]

There are still many people who do not accept the notion that women should be fully integrated into social and political life as self-evident. Furthermore, there has even been a certain setback in the achievements of the American feminist movement, on the issue of abortions, for example.

Feminism, which began with great momentum, has slowed down: many anti-feminist books have been written, some even by women, which advocate a return to the traditional, "natural" division of roles.[9] This trend has sought to overturn the achievements of the feminist movement. Anti-feminism is still very much in evidence; even now in the twenty-first century, it is liable to bring women back home and seriously limit their freedoms. Such erosion of women's rights would not be historically unique; similar reverses have occurred in the past. If anti-feminism has strong leadership and a well-formulated theory to provide moral justification for its position, it may achieve its objectives, even today. If women are not able to respond adequately to anti-feminism, their situation may well revert to its former state.

Merely opposing discriminatory and oppressive trends will not suffice to halt a deterioration of the situation. The reasons for women's inferior condition must also be understood and a way mapped to show how they might attain their rights.

To be effective, the methods of preventing oppression of women must penetrate to the heart of the problem – to the perception of the woman as being subhuman and an essentially non-rational creature. Therefore, the struggle against oppression of women should not be directed against men but rather against the philosophical theory that lies at the root of the oppression.

Because philosophy deals with abstractions, many think of it as an assortment of generalizations that are detached from the real, immediate problems of life, but this is not the case. The more philosophical, i.e., the more abstract an idea, the broader its base – so that it has greater power to build or destroy. Indeed, one finds that the same philosophical arguments and broad abstractions link all the oppressive acts toward women throughout history. These views are based on the contention that women do not act on the basis of rationality and thus cannot be included with men in the definition of humans as rational beings. This idea was expressed clearly by Aristotle, who thought that the differences between women and men, ensuing from the relative inferiority of women, were eternal and made it necessary that men govern women. Other philosophers as well, including Rousseau and Hegel, maintained that women were not capable of rational thought and that their responses were purely emotional, according to the proclivities of their hearts.

The perception of women as irrational creatures spread from philosophy to other disciplines and gave rise to severe limitations. Politically, until quite recently, women were denied civil rights, including the right to vote. This right is, as we know, denied to those who are incapable of rational judgment. Thus, children are not permitted to vote in elections because they have not yet acquired the knowledge needed for rational judgment on political issues; the mentally handicapped and the insane have either lost their mental abilities or never developed them and hence are not allowed to vote. In the past, the theoretical position that casts doubt on the ability of women to judge and make decisions led to the operative conclusion of denying them the right to vote in particular or to participate in political life altogether.[10]

The view that woman is a non-rational creature has also had repercussions in other spheres. In psychology and psychiatry, the normative woman is considered to be different from the normative man; the education system has prevented women from receiving an adequate education; in the economy, women have been assigned the tasks of homemaking and child care rather than earning a livelihood; in marriage, women have been obliged to bow to their husbands' wishes and settle for second place in the family.

The arguments that justified keeping women out of any activity outside the home all sprang from that philosophy which regarded women as inferior to men. Yet, women's attempts to challenge this definition using other philosophical arguments were rebuffed by the philosophical establishment on various grounds: feminism does not belong to the philosophical mainstream; philosophy is universal in approach and deals with humanity as a whole, whereas feminism deals with only part of the population.[11] This rejection begs the issue, since the questions feminism deals with are clearly philosophical. "Can women be included in the definition of mankind as rational creatures?" is, for example, a philosophical question. The contention that rejects this possibility appears in the doctrine of philosophers. Then, why should the opposing argument be excluded from philosophical debate?

The philosophical domain of ethics might examine the general principles regarding relations between men and women, and especially the issue of women's subordination to men. Ethics could also explore whether the good life for women would be different from that for men; whether the woman should aspire to happiness and the realization of her objectives and abilities or rather renounce these goals and always set the good of others before her own.

Political philosophy has suitable tools for clarifying the question of women's civil status – whether they should be as citizens with the same rights as men, or perhaps be accorded more privileges than men, or possibly be denied any rights at all. Is that political regime which is suitable and desirable for men also suitable for women? Is the most suitable regime for women one in which society would provide for all their needs on the assumption that women, by nature, are unable to care for themselves, or would it be better for women to live and function under conditions of economic and political freedom?

A search for the answers to these questions necessitates the prior investigation of more basic issues in the metaphysical and epistemological spheres. What is the nature of woman; what tools has she at her disposal for acquiring knowledge; and is she even capable of acquiring knowledge? Before we can determine what would be appropriate personally and politically, we must clarify whether there are substantive differences between females and males; whether a woman's cognitive ability is different from that of a man, based perhaps on intuition or emotion; and whether women are emotional and intuitive by nature and are not capable of rational thought or objective judgment. Metaphysics can help clarify the nature of women – whether their observed qualities are innate and impervious to change and therefore essentially metaphysical, or rather are they acquired and thus contingent and open to modification.

The questions that arise here thus belong to various philosophical spheres, since in defining the nature of women or men we should not content ourselves with the partial explanations provided by psychology and sociology [what is woman] or history [what was woman]. The obviously philosophical question of what woman can and should be is of decisive importance; therefore, it is philosophy, more than any other discipline, that can provide a proper answer.

In its second phase, feminism began to deal with another question from the domain of political philosophy: what is the role of the state in creating conditions that would enable the integration of motherhood and career and the advancement of women in the spheres of employment and income. As in the case of relations of women and men, here, too, opinions are divided. Feminists agree that conditions must be created which would enable women both to realize their potential and to live well, but there is disagreement as to how to achieve these objectives. Three basic approaches may be discerned in the suggested political solutions of women's problems: a communist state, a welfare state, and a free state.

The first, radical approach, advocates the communist ideology. Despite the low standard of living and the inferior status of women under communist regimes, radical feminists believed that the communist state could resolve the problem of the oppression of women better than the capitalist state, with its free, competitive economy. They identified capitalism with a patriarchal system, with exploitation, and hierarchy.[12]

Like Marx and Engels before them, radical feminists argued that male control of capital is the source of their power to oppress women and that only a new, communist-feminist redistribution of capital would afford women an opportunity for real equality. Among those who thought that the communist state would provide the optimal solution to the problems of women was the French author and philosopher Simone de Beauvoir. She believed that even though a different social structure was not created in the Soviet Union, a communist regime could potentially provide a suitable solution. She held that the reason most women did not manage to free themselves of the shackles of the traditional feminine world and become the equals of men was because they did not receive the necessary support from their husbands or from society. She maintained that only in a society in which care of the children was placed in the hands of the community could motherhood be reconciled with a career.[13]

The second approach, upheld by most feminists, advocates a welfare state. The values of such a state are perceived as being more "feminine" in that they show more concern for the individual in need. According to the advocates of this approach, these values should be the guiding principles in the political realm.

Carol Gilligan has undertaken an examination of the moral reasoning of men and women in an attempt to demonstrate that women show more concern for others, and speak in a "different voice" from that of men. Gilligan poses the following moral dilemma to her respondents: Heinz's wife is dying of a rare form of cancer, and the doctors believe that only a medicine recently developed by the village pharmacist can cure her. The pharmacist demands $2,000 for the medicine, and Heinz, who cannot raise the required sum, must cope with the dilemma.

From the answers of her respondents and from the results of other studies, Gilligan concludes that women show more concern for others than do men. She believes that since this "feminine" approach can ensure a better, less aggressive world, it should be one of the governing political principles. According to Gilligan, the best solution for the Heinz dilemma would be to steal the medicine from its owner. (Politically, this solution would mean distribution according to need, and in this case, health needs.) As Gilligan sees it, the injury caused to the pharmacist (loss of property, i.e., violation of the principle of private property) is of lesser magnitude than the expected injury to Heinz's wife (loss of life), and the lesser evil is preferable to the greater one.[14]

In the political realm, this approach would amount to advocacy of an extensive welfare state, or a socialist or communist regime. Sylvia Ann Hewlett also agrees that "feminine," non-aggressive values should govern human behavior, and therefore she supports a state in which society fulfils the special needs of women regardless of their ability to pay. Supporters of the second approach believe that since the husbands of most working women do not share in the burden of homemaking and childcare, the solution lies in a welfare state. Increasing the role of the state in childcare and allocating benefits to working women would help the women combine motherhood and a career. On the other hand, the capitalist state, they say, does not offer any solution for this problem.[15]

At the close of the twentieth century, the average salary of women was 59% that of men, primarily due to the fact that women were concentrated in professions such as nurses, secretaries, or librarians. Women's salaries should be determined through state intervention. The state should classify all occupations according to their value and should, for example, compel private business owners to pay women and men equal pay for work of equal value. If secretarial work were classified as equal in value to plumbing, workers in both professions would be entitled to the same wage. This step harbors long-range social benefits – this way women who work for low salaries would rise above the poverty line. As individual workers, women are helpless; because of their limited skills and the large supply of female laborers available, women carry little weight in the labor market. Therefore, women must organize and exploit their collective power in order to achieve higher pay, improved working conditions, and assistance in child care – state subsidized childcare workers or daycare centers.[16] The demand for state assistance is solidified by arguing that the decision to bring a child into the world has not only a private benefit but a public one as well; children are the next generation, and in them rests the future of the nation; moreover, it is known that neglected children grow up to be problematic rather than productive citizens.[17]

The third approach is completely different from those already outlined. It argues that government intervention would actually harm women's welfare and their prospects for achieving equality and that the best political solution for both women and men would be found in a state with a free economy, i.e., laissez faire capitalism. The nineteenth century philosopher, John Stuart Mill, a man of the classical-liberal school, is among the advocates of this approach. Mill opposed men's political control over women and labeled it the tyranny of nations, which in other respects were civilized.[18]

Advocates of political freedom argue that only a policy of liberty, rather than coercion, would give women the opportunity to establish their worth in the labor market. According to advocates of this approach, women need to diversify their career choices and then demonstrate that they are capable of fulfilling them successfully. As they see it, feminists are wrong if they say that women should not take the trouble to learn other skills, encouraging them to remain in their traditional occupations. It would be a mistake to aspire to improve women's wages by legal proceedings against private employers. Such an approach, argue its detractors, would reinforce the opinion that women are less ambitious and capable than men – and this, of course, is something feminists ought to reject out of hand.

The demand that forbids a private employer to pay a secretary a wage lower than that of a plumber is based on the false premise that work has a value or a price even if there is no one around to pay it, i.e., that there can be values without those to make value judgments. This belief is mistaken seeing as when value is divorced from the evaluation of those involved in some transaction, voluntary exchange (which takes place according to the judgment of each buyer and seller) is not possible. There is no reason to believe that if only one component needing correction is changed, then all else will remain as before. In the political domain, every change in one area makes it necessary to relate to the entire complex of all its ramifications. It is certain that assigning values and imposing wages will not stop with setting the value of women's work and that the principle which enables intervention for women's benefit will also lead to intervention in other spheres.

In doing so, government officials assessing the value of occupations in which most women are concentrated would also be determining whether soccer players are worth more or less than cancer researchers. The construction of a strict hierarchy of occupations according to their value would constitute a real threat to economic freedom and therefore also to welfare in its broadest sense.[19]

Indeed, for the proposed political principle to be taken seriously, it must not ignore any relevant aspect. Gilligan's example discussed above spoke of two people – the inventor of the medicine and the patient who needs it. The viewpoint of the inventor must not be ignored, as Gilligan does when she fails to see him as a party with moral demands or any rights at all. Even, if ostensibly, it seemed that the sick person's problem had been alleviated (as would be the case with the distress of a hungry person who stole bread from the baker), when advocating a political principle, it is not enough to provide an immediate solution and achieve an improvement in an individual situation.

It is also necessary to weigh the more, far-reaching consequences of putting the principle into practice: will this decision achieve the desired result – greater welfare and alleviated distress – not only in one instance but everywhere and at all times? Would it be worthwhile for the man and woman whose immediate needs are met in a specific instance to live in a state in which distribution according to need constitutes a determining principle? Is it not possible to resolve such problems as that of Heinz and his sick wife and still respect the right to private property of the inventor of the medicine?

This book attempts to fill a void that exists in feminist literature in the political sphere; most feminist literature deals with the individual trees without seeing the forest and without examining the overall ramifications of proposed solutions.

An investigation of political questions such as reducing or increasing government intervention is crucial for women's struggle. These questions have implications for the quality of life of women as persons who consume food, need clothing and a roof over their heads, seek an education, and require medical care and recreation. The discussion of the proposed solutions aims to achieve well-being for women, not mere equality.

Discussion of a political solution for women's issues necessitates consideration of the female nature – the essence of the differences between women and men.

Chapter 2 will examine the assumptions that have caused women's roles to be restricted to the home and family and the denial or limitation of their civil rights.

Chapter 3 will be devoted to a discussion of the relations that would be desirable between women and men and will ask whether women's traditional role serves the interests of the other members of the family.

Political solutions suggested by feminists will be examined in Chapter 4: does a policy of total or partial intervention afford women the best possibilities for their advancement and welfare or would a state that respected the rights of individuals, including private property rights, be preferable?

Most political and theoretical writing has placed men at the center. The discussion has focused on man, and the place of women has gone unnoticed. The word "man" has a double meaning: a human being in general and specifically a male. Here, matters will be presented from a feminine perspective.

This book, however, is directed at a male audience as well, because it raises questions that necessitate male consideration in addition to a willingness to change fundamental perceptions. Males can also profit from the historical experience of women; the fate of women throughout human history has lessons for men as well – hence the title of this book with its implicit admonition: We've Already Been There.

2. The Nature of Women

The Determinist View
of Feminine Attributes

Aristotle and other philosophers, among them Rousseau, Kant, and Hegel, argued that women differ from men regarding their ways of thinking, behavior, and personality, and that these attributes are set and immutable.[1] Among those who agree with them are psychologists, theologians, and even feminists.

In previous centuries, it was argued, primarily by philosophers and theologians, that women were governed by instincts and emotions and not by intelligence, and, therefore, were not completely human and were not suited to govern or to be citizens. It was commonly thought that women's intellect was inferior to that of men. Since it was assumed that the search for abstract truth, principles, or axioms in science was not a feminine characteristic, it was understood that women were not creative. The reality that women had not made a significant contribution in any social or cultural sphere was taken as decisive evidence in this regard. Expressions of talent, keenness of perception, or outstanding intellectual ability were perceived as excellence in men, whereas in women they were considered unfeminine qualities.[2]

Failure to realize their potential was not considered pathological in women but as normal womanliness. Women were thought willing, by their very nature, to live through others (especially their husbands and children) by sacrificing their own goals.

These perceptions that prevailed in previous centuries also exist today. Even today, women are considered to be intuitive and emotional. Many human qualities are defined as characteristic of only one of the sexes and constitutive of its identity. When a member of one sex displays a quality typical of members of the other sex, the phenomenon is considered as going "against nature." If a woman chooses to engage in an athletic, political, or intellectual activity or in the same pursuits as her father, Freud interpreted her predilection as masculine behavior. According to him, her choice in this case was inauthentic and did not suit her sex.[3] Even if here and there one discerns differences in terminology between early psychoanalytic theory and that of today, the latter has not ceased to emphasize the differences it finds between the personalities and functions of the two sexes. This extends to parenthood as well. Freud and his followers believed that the woman-mother primarily symbolized love and tenderness, whereas the man-father symbolized power and authority. The woman was perceived by psychoanalysts as passive, masochistic, the source of love in the home, and capable, at most, of being a helpmate to her husband. The man was perceived as active, masterful, and able to cope with the world around him.[4]

Biologists are also party to this perception of the innate difference between men and women. Contemporary scientific studies reinforce the images, inherited from the past, of masculinity and femininity: masculinity is described as being influenced by male hormones and in terms of sexual initiative, high intelligence, and the desire for vocational success; whereas femininity, in the absence of male hormones, is devoid of these "male" qualities.

Femininity is linked to sexual passivity, lower intelligence, and motherly tendencies, and hence, to the absence of vocational ambition.[5] It is not only those who would limit women to their homes and families who share the almost dichotomous perception of innate "masculine" and "feminine" characteristics. There are also feminists who argue that women, by nature, like to cooperate with others and are less competitive, that their ways of thinking are essentially different from those of men, that they are more sensitive, devoted, and "better" than men.[6]

Which qualities of women are innate and which are the product of society? We must clarify whether feminine qualities, as described above, are inherent and essential, in which case they cannot be changed, or whether they stem from social influences and pressures, i.e. whether they are acquired, in which case, when social patterns change, they too may change.

"Women are Not Creative by Nature and Do Not Excel in Any Sphere"

Historically, for many centuries, there were relatively few significant female creative accomplishments. If this lack of excellence was derived from social circumstances, we cannot use the past to predict the future. On the contrary, it may be assumed that if social and political conditions change, then female creativity will expand as well.

Like men, women cannot cope with existential or intellectual problems in the absence of suitable conditions for creativity. The development of revolutionary theories and the suggestion of innovative solutions for existential problems are manifestations of the intellectual capacity of man or woman for unique, independent accomplishment that is beyond the familiar. Sometimes such accomplishments attest to the personal courage needed to publicly challenge conventional perceptions. In order for women or men to publicize their unique ideas, they must be confident in their intellectual powers and judgment. The possibility of learning and working and the opportunity to acquire suitable vocational training and adequate work experience are essential for men and women to achieve new, innovative accomplishments.

For example, a woman from the orthodox Jewish community is not allowed to study sacred texts and will therefore never become a "Torah giant"; a woman who is forbidden to learn jurisprudence cannot have a successful law career; a woman who is not allowed to serve in positions of governmental authority cannot become a prominent stateswoman; if, in the past, men in the theater also played the roles of women, a woman could not become an outstanding actress. It is not enough for a woman to possess exceptional abilities and supreme determination; to succeed she must be given the opportunity to learn and implement her abilities in the workplace. Throughout history, all those conditions, which were critical for the development of women as creative beings, did not usually exist.

Convincing the Woman
of Her "Inferiority"

The creative person must have faith in his or her intellectual abilities, but women were not encouraged to have such faith. The creative person does not accept the opinions of others without question, but women were brought up to believe that obedience was a feminine virtue.

Stifling a woman's confidence in her intelligence makes it easier for those who try to limit the spheres in which she can be active. There is a causal relationship between convincing the woman of her intellectual inferiority and her willingness to accept the constraints that are imposed upon her without question.

In previous centuries, the woman was brought up to believe that her existence was of lesser importance and that it was her destiny to serve a more noble being. Her entire upbringing was geared to convince her that she did not belong to the sex intended by nature to be creative because she lacked suitable intellectual ability; that she should not aspire to a long-range professional career, often essential in making a serious breakthrough in some sphere; that her only role, preordained, was care of the home and the children. All other roles she was to leave in the hands of men.

Rousseau, more than any other thinker, was instrumental in barring women from any creative endeavor except for their roles in the home and family. Rousseau – as well as many others, including Kant, Hegel, and many theologians – based his conclusions on assumptions that cast doubt upon the abilities of women. He believed that the intellectual abilities of women were inferior to those of men; that women had a better grasp of practical details but were not capable of understanding general principles; that although capable of learning, women did not have the serious intellectual capacities demanded by activities in the sciences, philosophy, and even in the arts; that women were guided by their unique and personal experience and not by universal truths; that women were not capable of deriving abstract ideas from concrete cases; and that women's inability to focus on intellectual ratiocination was a fixed characteristic. Rousseau claimed that women, governed by their emotions, were less rational than men and were thus less competent to participate in all areas of social activities, including political life. The conclusion to be drawn from these assumptions was that only men, who control their emotions and are motivated by their intellect, were capable of managing societal affairs rationally and objectively.[1] Since their nature closes off the paths to intellectual excellence, women would not derive any benefit from higher, more advanced education; such education would be contrary to their nature even if they were to receive it. Rather, they must focus on the sphere that suits their nature, i.e., the home and family.[2]

Therefore, women must be trained from childhood to submit to authority, and thus, will never consider this authority to be a burden. Girls will learn that dependence is a natural state for women. Education to accept authority will lead to obedience, necessary for women who are forever subject to the authority of men.[3]

Religious ideology joins this philosophic doctrine. Classical monotheism opposes any possibility of women participating in making decisions and in managing community life. In this, there is almost no difference between Jewish orthodoxy and conservative Catholicism, or radical Islam.

The traditional sexual division of roles – man as ruler and woman as ruled – is justified by reference to the biblical account of creation: man was created first "in God's image," and woman was created from his rib; therefore, man's primacy and authority are self-evident.

According to the Jewish faith, God created woman to relieve man's loneliness. She is not a being in her own right, but rather her purpose resides in her spouse.[4] She was created in order to please man, to accept his rule even when it causes her injury.[5]

Even though the woman is man's companion, she must not see her husband as her friend but rather as her master who rules her; if a woman will not voluntarily act like a maidservant, then he will be her master despite her wishes.[6]

Religious ideology dictated exclusion of the woman from almost all spheres of activities except those connected to the home and family. The Jewish religion assigns all the important roles to men and accords differential rights to the sexes in all spheres – social, familial, legal, and military. For example, women are not allowed to serve as judges in rabbinical courts, even at the lowest judicial level; women are disqualified from giving testimony on any matter that necessitates two lawful witnesses. Women's emotionalism, it is contended, prevents her from serving in these positions – her emotionalism is liable to cause her to err in her judgment.

According to traditional Judaism, a woman's place is in the home; she should not be seen in the streets of the city. Moses Maimonides decreed that the husband must allow his wife to leave the home only once or twice a month, one of those times being her obligatory visit to the ritual bath following her menstrual period.[7]

To a large extent, the attitude of Christianity toward the woman comes from Judaism. Divine authority is delegated to the man – the father, the husband; his mastery is dictatorial and knows no bounds. Like Aristotle, Paul, too, advised the woman to act with humility and silence, as befitted her inferior position. In the epistle to the Ephesians, St. Paul expressed his opinion about the relations between a husband and wife thusly:

> *Husbands, love your wives, even as Christ also loved the church... Therefore as the church is subject unto Christ, so let the wives be to their own husbands in everything...*

When a woman is contemptuous of her husband by refusing to obey him, she opposes the law of God who wanted woman to be subject to her husband because he is nobler and more perfect than woman, having been created in God's image, whereas she was created in man's.

In the seventeenth century, Benedict, the prominent preacher from Lyon, wrote that the woman who seeks to lord over the household contrary to her husband's wishes is a sinner; she should not go against her husband's commands since she is subject to him by virtue of the laws of man and God.[8]

Christianity assumes that women are not allowed to speak in public. Paul said that it was shameful for women to speak in church; if they want to understand something, they must ask their husbands at home.[9]

The same situation is seen in many Muslim countries as well. In the east, women sometimes sat behind a curtain, through which they could see but not be seen, or else they were obliged to cover their mouths. The veil prevented women from speaking in public and essentially removed them from public life.[10]

It is known that opinions and habits that are acquired during childhood are deeply rooted, and that it takes many years to displace them. Women raised in religious Catholic, Muslim, or Orthodox Jewish families cannot easily escape their domestic roles, since these are sanctified by the canons of their religions, which define the essence of married life and motherhood.[11]

Women educated in particularly religious settings are taught absolute obedience, since religion forbids questioning supreme authority. The message of blind obedience to authority is conveyed in the biblical narrative of Abraham who is commanded to take his son, Isaac, to Mount Moriah and sacrifice him to God. This difficult command is not explained to Abraham, who is forced to be satisfied with the fact that it is a divine edict, and therefore, just. Abraham must prove his faith and obey the command without question.

The young orthodox Jewish woman has no access to secular literature, which is critical of religious writings and rabbinical literature. Preventing her from becoming acquainted with opposing attitudes and alternative perceptions has also contributed to her unquestioning acceptance of the religious precepts that constrain women.

Social Limitations and Prohibitions

Until quite recently, women were not allowed into most spheres of activities outside the home, not only because of limiting religious edicts. Separation of the sexes in the public domain was not the exclusive notion of religious circles; secular society also segregated the world of women from that of men. This division expressed itself in the existence of separate institutions for men – social clubs, schools, and work places. Women thus found themselves shut out from important areas of activities, and they were denied the opportunity to prove to themselves and others that they were not less capable than men. Women did not dare to deviate from their traditional roles primarily, because they were kept unaware of their abilities and hence of the realization that they might have other choices. The occupational separation was self-perpetuating, because women had no way of discovering that the jobs reserved for men were not too difficult and could also be performed by women. The separate existences did not allow women to realize that men are not necessarily wiser, more courageous, or stronger than women. Women could not appraise their own capacities, because they were completely unfamiliar with masculine pursuits.[12]

Until recent decades, the aspirations of girls for a different future received little encouragement in most societies. They were brought up to be passive, to wait patiently, and to obey, first their parents and later their husbands. And indeed, obedience and acceptance of fate continued even after marriage, because marital matches were so arranged that the woman was always inferior to her husband and therefore would not dare to oppose his control over her. In almost all spheres, great or small, the woman was supposed to be inferior to the man: she was shorter, her education and experience in life were less broad, her occupation was of lower rank, and her vocational training was less extensive, her professional experience and involvement in community matters were more limited. These spheres were open to the man, her husband, whereas she was excluded. The husband was also more experienced than his wife in sexual matters; she was taught to protect her modesty as a supreme value, and great importance was placed on her virginity, which she was instructed to guard until her marriage. The wider experience of the husband also stemmed from the fact that he was usually older than his wife. She was so young and inexperienced at the time of her marriage, and what was actually immaturity and childishness was mistakenly thought to be the result of inherent differences between the sexes.[13]

Simone de Beauvoir claims that even if there were women who were naturally more intelligent than their spouses, because of their lack of education and work experience, they were still incapable of formulating their ideas and reasoning logically. Therefore, even if their husbands were less astute, they could easily rule over their wives and prove themselves right.[14]

The Use of Force in the Family

Although every means was used to prove to women that they were naturally inferior to men and that it was natural for men to dominate them, women did not always willingly accept this subordinate role.

In the past, researchers tended to paint a picture of social harmony, according to which women acquiesced in their subordinate positions, but the facts indicate that men's control over women was not achieved easily. This is attested to by violence toward women within the family, which was intended to achieve blind obedience. While such violence did not characterize every family, it was widespread and not only among the uneducated and poor classes, but also among middle-class families.

The threat of the use of force on the part of husbands and fathers proved effective enough in enabling men to control women. The threat of divorce, for example, was sufficient to force a woman to behave as her husband desired and to limit her power in the family, especially if she could not support herself, or if because of law or custom, she was not entitled to inherit or manage property.[15]

Men have needed to use force against women because the latter knew from personal experience that it is not so that all women are inferior to all men: the woman who is raised alongside her brother and who lives alongside her husband may discover that she is not less capable than they are. According to Simone de Beauvoir, a woman who lives among men will not easily accept the unquestioned superiority of men. Women, who for various reasons, have been forced to manage on their own for certain periods of time are sometimes surprised to learn that they have abilities that they never knew existed. They take charge, make decisions, and bear the burden alone. They are angry that when their husbands return, they are forced to revert to passivity and incompetency.[16] But they no longer accept their subservience and inferiority as self-evident.

Political Limitations and Prohibitions

The inferior position of women within the family and the physical injury that they suffered at the hands of men was reinforced by the law. The law did not punish those who used violence against women in the family; such violence was perceived as "different" from other crimes.[17]

Until the recent past, laws were usually created, interpreted, and put into practice by men. It has been shown that the cultural preferences of those who administer the legal system – judges, attorneys, and policemen – influence their interpretation of the law. It is enough to note how the legal system treated rapists or abusive husbands until relatively recently. Examples are abundant. Judges in India, for example, were known to refrain from punishing husbands who murdered their wives simply because their dowries were inadequate.[18] By contrast, the legal system punished women severely. In the United States and Great Britain, until recently, women who killed in self-defense were sentenced to life imprisonment, whereas, in the past, men were let off with relatively light punishment for murdering their wives.[19]

Domestic violence toward women was not addressed because the woman was considered to be her husband's property, and therefore, he was permitted to do with her as he pleased. Women also lacked independent standing before the law. John Stuart Mill notes that the legal status of slaves in the United States during the eighteenth century was derived from the legal status of women; until the twentieth century, women were denied the right to participate in political and social life. The American Constitution did not grant women the right to vote. If a woman was married, she was considered non-existent in the eyes of the law. She was denied the right to property or even to the wages she might have earned by her labor.[20] Until recently, American law upheld the prohibition on giving loans to women for business purposes or acquiring cars and homes.[21] Until not so long ago, in several states in the United States and in many other countries, women were not entitled to sell their property without the approval of their husbands, so that the latter, in effect, become co-owners of the property. In France, for example, until thirty years ago, a married woman could not open her own bank account without her husband's signature.[22]

Deprived of many rights, women lacked the tools to act to change their situation. They were denied the right to work in many fields, to own property, to speak in public, to vote in elections, to hold political office, or even to control their own power of reproduction (due to anti-abortion legislation). The absence of rights in one sphere prevented women from acting to achieve rights in another. Thus, without the right to own property or to speak in public, women could not struggle for female suffrage.

This right, in turn, would have enabled women to try to change the laws which constrained them in the professional and educational arenas and to try to repeal the law which denied them the freedom of deciding for themselves how many children they wanted.[23]

Woman's confinement to the home stemmed in large part from explicit prohibitions[24] that were enacted under the influence of philosophical perceptions concerning the inferiority of women.

Education, Rousseau argued, corrupted women, since it diverted their attention from their most sacred obligations. Napoleon, inspired by Rousseau, instituted a special education program for girls, in which religious studies were the most prominent element. He thought that women should be raised to believe, not to think, and that they could be convinced of their proper place in the social order through religion. Along with religious studies, three quarters of the curriculum was devoted to sewing and the remainder to courses in nursing and cooking; if necessary, women would know how to replace a servant unable to work.

In Napoleon's opinion, the education of girls had only one objective: to train them to be devoted wives and efficient housekeepers. The aim was to avoid distracting the woman-to-be from her natural duties, and therefore, she should not be afforded an education for its own sake, since this might make her arrogant and ambitious to exploit her knowledge for professional goals.

Later, when women were already permitted to receive an education, the purpose of education was still seen in terms of augmenting women's training for their domestic roles. An inspiration for this attitude was Voltaire, who maintained that any woman who neglected her obligations and devoted herself to science should be censured.

In other words, the woman could learn, but she was not allowed to put her learning into practice. A woman could not aspire to a status any higher than the confidential advisor of a man in high position, since she was forbidden access to so many things.[25]

In earlier centuries, the situation in the United States was not much different. In 1873, the Supreme Court decreed that according to the Constitution, a young woman named Myra Bradwell was not entitled to practice law. Judge Joseph P. Bradley wrote that in his opinion:

> *The natural and proper timidity and delicacy that belongs to the female sex evidently unfits it for many of the occupations of civil life. The paramount destiny and mission of women are to fulfill the noble and benign office of wife and mother. This is the law of the Creator.*

It was only in 1928 that the first female law student was admitted to Columbia University.[26]

Until they were abrogated in 1967, legal restrictions in the United States prevented women from serving as judges, practicing medicine, teaching, or engaging in the fields of banking or insurance.[27]

Since for so many generations women were not accorded the possibility of acquiring a proper education and were prohibited from participating in so many fields of endeavor, their true abilities cannot be judged on the basis of the past. The contention that women's creativity is inferior by nature to that of men is inappropriate: no comparison may be made between the situation and activities of the two sexes because they have been subject to such disparate conditions. Contrary to the case of men, women's full development was beset by obstacles.[28] In 1977, the American Department of Labor listed 20,000 existing occupations world-wide,[29] many of which had been in existence long before. While all these possibilities were open to men, women were confined to household tasks. Simone de Beauvoir observed that men were free to become either heads of state or coal miners, scientists, or builders, whereas women could be only mothers and housewives. The girl would become a wife, mother, and grandmother. She would take care of the household exactly as her mother had done before her. At the age of twelve, the story of her life had already been determined.[30]

Constraining Social Norms in the Second Half of the Twentieth Century

During the twentieth century, women were gradually accorded more civil rights. In some states, they were given the right to vote and were permitted to study and work in most professions. Despite this, women have not yet achieved outstanding accomplishments in all spheres of endeavor. Some conclude that this is because women, by nature, lack the capacity for excellence, creativity, or innovation. Otherwise, why has there not been a large number of women to seize the opportunities which became available to them?

Those who claim that only women are to blame, do not attach sufficient importance to the mediating effects of the political regime and the educational and social patterns that still assign women secondary roles. At first glance, it would seem that with the removal of explicit formal prohibitions, women ought to have been able to make careers of work and attain impressive achievements. But the environment has done almost everything to steer them into traditional channels. For example, in the United States and in other Western countries, women have more legal opportunities than in the past. However, the government still has the power to encourage or prevent women from working, not only by employing explicit prohibitions but also via indirect means. This possibility was indeed used, and will be dealt with at greater length in the political section of this book. (Because women in the United States have been accorded more legal rights to study and work than in other countries, and since its population is large, most of the following facts and examples will be taken from there.)

In order for women to succeed in all social areas, it is not only crucial for suitable political conditions to be in place, but also a conducive, social-cultural climate, which would not ostracize them because of their activities. Their success must be regarded as legitimate and not as a challenge to social mores. A woman with a successful career should not be considered masculine, deviant, peculiar, and as betraying her true, natural role. Not every woman is endowed with the necessary willpower, determination, and devotion required of those who swim against the current. Precisely when the institutions of higher learning and most spheres of endeavor were opened to American women, the expression "career woman" acquired a negative connotation.[31]

In her book, *Of Woman Born*, Adrienne Rich observes that a woman can indeed be anything she really wants to be if she is ready to struggle to set her own priorities in the face of all cultural expectations and to persevere tenaciously against all opposition.[32]

Socialization results not from isolated acts or attempts to persuade but rather from the impact of mutually consistent, regular messages, as well as the absence of other divergent influences.[33] In the period following the Second World War in the United States, the tendency to limit women from realizing their aspirations was widespread; tremendous social pressures still prevented them from seeking their place in the world through studies and work and prodded them toward resigning themselves to lives which revolved around the home and family.

First and foremost, the girl's parents taught her about a woman's proper place. They taught her that when she grew up she would not be responsible for her own life, and that her standard of living would not depend upon her work but rather upon that of her husband.

During the 1950s, parents still raised their daughters more for marriage and family than for personal development and creative endeavors. The young woman was encouraged to think that finding a husband was her most important goal in life, since only through him could she achieve social status and acquire a personal identity; only marriage could bring her advantages. Most parents did not seriously consider their daughter's studies and her professional future, nor did they afford her the same decent education and professional training deemed proper for her brother.

Even if the girl received a good education and treatment equal to her brother materially, still the parents evinced less interest in her grades, valued her achievements less highly, and gave less encouragement to her professional aspirations.

The following statement of a woman who grew up during the 1950s reflects the educational attitude prevalent at that time:

> *I felt from as long as I can remember that my brother was treated more generously, lovingly, and unequivocally than I... My mother did not think that my daydreams could come true. Her lack of faith in me and amused (not exactly cruel) attitude toward my ambitions made me very angry.*[34]

Even a mother who exhibited sincere concern for her daughter's future thought it prudent to make her a "real woman," so that society would more readily accept her. The books chosen for her convey the message that suitable areas of endeavor for her were cooking, sewing, or housework. At that time, a girl would not be told that she must prepare herself seriously for a profession and a career, but rather for marriage. In contrast, the boy was not (and is not) taught to see marriage as his main objective in life. For him, economic and professional attainments would confer social status and success in his adult life.

Men's serious attitude towards work as defining their identity is reflected in research on men who grew up during that period. When asked whether they were jealous of women's opportunity to be supported economically by their husbands, the overwhelming majority of male respondents replied that they were not jealous, and they expressed vigorous opposition to the idea of being supported by others. In their view, a man could not have much self-esteem if he did not support himself.[35]

While a profession, studies, activities, and achievement were concepts considered foreign to the world of women, beauty was the only sphere in which women could legitimately excel. The social message conveyed to women (and to men) was that men are judged according to their deeds and achievements, whereas women were judged based on their external appearance. A girl or woman was valued first and foremost for her attractive external appearance, and this is what would bring her success.

Indeed, the prettier the girl, the greater her success with the opposite sex. When choosing a girlfriend, teenage boys first looked for an appealing appearance. In contrast, girls considered the most important quality in their male friends to be intelligence. They also used more criteria in choosing their friends, including academic proficiency, athletic ability, and leadership.

The desire for a beautiful appearance need not hinder ambition, the desire to succeed, and serious interest in a career in and of itself, but it does interfere when it comes at their expense, and when the capacity to act is replaced by the ability to attract.[36]

Because of these divergent messages, boys and girls turned to different directions in their development. The male planned his pursuits at an early age and examined alternatives in order to find the vocation best suited to his abilities, interests, temperament, and needs. The female, on the other hand, concentrated on improving her external appearance in anticipation of her marriage. It was found that girls who went to college between 1945-1960 did not show serious interest in anything except marriage and motherhood.[37] They saw no point in investing effort in acquiring an education since it would not have any practical application or continuation in their future lives. They regarded careers as an impediment to married life and raising a family. They showed no interest in many spheres, such as nuclear physics, modern art, other cultures, or philosophy, because they did not expect to make a career in these areas. (In the last few decades, under the influence of feminism, parents have begun to encourage their daughters to acquire a better education and professional training, but the absence of success in these areas is more easily overlooked in daughters than in sons.)[38]

Even if the woman works until her marriage, because she lacks suitable professional training, she is sentenced to remain at the lower levels of her profession; a vicious cycle ensues: professional inferiority strengthens her desire to find herself a husband and provider.[39]

Many other factors were added to the girl's upbringing in her parents' home that reinforced the message about the desirable division of roles. American educators tended not to train and encourage females to participate actively in the wider society; they urged girls to study subjects such as home economics, whereas the boys were directed towards the study of physics and mathematics. Women were less likely to study such subjects, because they had been raised on the myth that science and mathematics were the exclusive purview of men.[40]

During that period, textbooks rarely mentioned women who were active outside the home. The texts that were studied in schools always described women as apron-wearing mothers, whose aspirations were completely centered on the home and family and who had no interest whatsoever in engaging in any profession. Books which alluded to feminine professions usually mentioned service and care-giving professions such as nursing and teaching or glamorous activities such as modeling, dancing, or acting, in which the body was an important element.[41]

Politicians at that time also supported the traditional sexual division of roles. In a 1955 commencement address at Smith College, Adlai Stevenson dismissed the desire of educated women to play their own political part in "the crises of the age." He said that woman's political job was:

> *to help her husband find values that will give purpose to his specialized daily chores...to teach her children the uniqueness of each individual human being. This assignment for you, as wives and mothers, you can do in the living room with a baby in your lap or in the kitchen with a can opener in your hand. If you're clever, maybe you can even practice your saving arts on that unsuspecting man while he's watching television. I think there is much you can do about our crisis in the humble role of housewife. I could wish you no better vocation.*[42]

In other words, in Stevenson's opinion, women were not expected to act independently at all but rather to assist those doing the real work, from behind the scenes.

In France, this approach was expressed explicitly by President Poincare in a speech at the opening ceremony of a high school for girls on the eve of World War I:

> *We do not wish, for the majority of them, that this dream [a career] become a reality... It is not to the*

courtroom or the lecture hall that we are trying to direct our pupils. Our goal...is that they remain loving daughters, later to become devoted wives and attentive mothers.[43]

Such examples demonstrate that no real change had occurred in that social climate in America and Europe, which did not look favorably upon educated or career-seeking women.[44]

In the United States during the 1950s and 1960s, women also heard from economists that nothing could compare with the traditional family, that is, the combination of breadwinner and housewife, for economic efficiency. A man could devote himself to his work and build a prosperous career, because his wife had freed him from household concerns.[45] Literature and the cinema also painted no picture of the woman other than as mother and homemaker. A woman with professional accomplishments was represented as a rare, anomalous phenomenon.

In both the United States and Europe, women were urged to limit their professional aspirations and refrain from unequivocal devotion to their studies or their careers. An intellectual woman was not considered attractive by men because her success threatened their supremacy. Women were led to believe that men did not like "masculine," overly intelligent women; that independent women who were too daring, educated, or intelligent repel men. Women learned that they should be content with moderate success and not dare to aspire too high, because if they went too far, they might get hurt.[46]

For the man, there was no contradiction between his full human development and professional success and his being a male. Men strive for success, wealth, fame, and admiration simultaneously. But talented and successful women pay a price for this in their personal lives – either they do not marry or they have difficulty in preserving the family unit intact.

Today as well, many men openly admit that if their wives were to earn more than they or achieve greater recognition, it would hurt their self-image. This attitude causes women to avoid investing maximum effort in their work so as not to attain outstanding results or earn the highest wages; a woman knows that at the end of the long and difficult road to her own success awaits her injured husband.

In order to appear more "feminine," women and girls in previous decades were known to conceal their talents and abilities and withdraw altogether from the mainstream of thought, participation, and accomplishment in society.[47] In coeducational high schools and colleges, females of the recent past avoided speaking in class for fear of being classified as "clever"; they refrained from defeating males in competitive games and from receiving high grades.

All the social elements that contributed to keeping women in traditional roles were augmented by the full weight of Freudian theory. Freud's ideas were widely disseminated through the media,[48] and many men and women in the United States and in Western Europe embraced his theory concerning sexual differences and the distinction between the roles of the mother and the father.

At the time, beliefs prevalent in previous centuries concerning the inferiority of women and their roles began to receive scientific reinforcement. According to Freud, all women suffered from penis envy, and small girls saw themselves as deformed boys. When a girl saw the sexual organ of the boy, she immediately understood her own "imperfection." She did not accept this inferiority of hers but rebelled instead. She coveted the male sexual organ. This caused a trauma whose solution could take the neurotic form of searching for the lost penis by imitating masculine activity (i.e., aspiring to a career) or else the more acceptable form of wanting a male child, an infant son who would bring the lost penis with him. The mother could transfer the ambition, which she was obliged to repress, to her son.

Freud suggested that "normal" femininity was only achieved when the woman forewent her personal goals and any "originality" she possessed to fulfill herself through identification with the actions and objectives of her husband or son. But when the woman saw her work as a career, her ambition was explained as an instinct based on penis envy, not as an expression of authentic femininity. Any attempt by the woman to engage in creative work was considered scandalous, imitative ("like the men"), or an evasion of the "real" tasks of mature womanliness, which are marriage and motherhood.[49]

If a woman sought emotional assistance because she felt miserable in her role as mother and homemaker and sought to give her life meaning through some serious endeavor, Freud's followers directed her to seek out the reason for her unhappiness within herself; they believed that the problem lay within her and not in the surrounding world which barred her way to development and participation. According to Freud, women were not dissatisfied as a result of their inferior social status or their exhausting work burden, but rather, because of an emotional neurosis.[50]

Support in the United States for the attitude that the female role is based chiefly on motherhood is supplied by what Betty Friedan refers to as the "feminine mystique." According to this mystique, the highest value for women and their sole obligation is to realize their capacity for motherhood; the root of women's problems in the past has been jealousy of men and the attempt to imitate them instead of accepting their own nature and resigning themselves to being women whose main occupation centered around the home and family. In the role of wife, vital in its own right for fulfillment of her femininity, the woman is not guaranteed full satisfaction; only motherhood enables the woman to develop to her utmost. The woman must be a mother, not from time to time but rather twenty-four hours a day.

The anthropologist Margaret Mead was one of the chief supporters of this approach. She believed that women would lose their femininity if they sought self-realization beyond their biological role as mothers. The most important accomplishment of a woman was the birth of her children, and this is her chief glory.[51]

Perhaps the most important reason that so many women avoided going out to work was the fear that they might not succeed in combining a full-time job or career with raising children and homemaking. This attitude stemmed from the conception of "complete motherhood," which at that time was considered essential for raising children successfully.

After World War II, a new generation of experts continued to encourage mothers to raise their children in the spirit of the ideal that there was no proper substitute for a mother's love and concern, and therefore, mothers should raise their own children. The experts believed that, in the long run, the worst natural mother was preferable to the best nursery school teacher.

The "complete mother" cult was still present in the United States only two decades ago. Its main message was that full-time work does not go hand in hand with good motherhood. In the 20th century, it was still thought that the mother could raise children with superior potential with her attentiveness, emotional sensitivity, and constant presence.

In France, the message that resonated up until recently was that a married woman must dissociate herself from any aspiration to be economically independent; otherwise, her children would be the victims of her ambition. It was thought that the woman must sacrifice her career or else risk harming her children. For decades, French women's magazines extolled the stereotypical images of the good mother who sits at home, and have warned of the dangers in store for the child whose mother has abandoned him or her by going out to work. Many psychologists and educational counselors have expressed themselves in these terms in popular journals and afforded "scientific" legitimacy to the demand that women confine themselves to their traditional roles.[52]

The picture that emerges from such counsel is this: the woman must choose between living alone, without love or a home or children or a caring companion, with her work as her only comfort in life, or else, for the sake of the joys of love, she must devote herself to her home and children and forego any professional aspirations. Support for this view was exemplified by many famous creative women who chose not to raise families or bring children into the world in order to achieve success in their field of endeavor. The four great female authors – George Eliot, Emily Bronte, Jane Austen, and Charlotte Bronte – were cited as cautionary examples.[53]

In light of this either-or stand concerning the opportunities available to women, it is not surprising that so many women chose family life as their only goal in life, whereas men could raise families and also devote themselves to a career at the same time.

Many social messages combined to deter girls and women from working outside the home, excelling in their studies and at work, and striving for accomplishment. When, despite this, some women were ready to tackle "masculine" professions, they often came up against opposition in their places of work. Many men prevented women from entering traditional masculine domains such as law and medicine, and many opposed appointing women to executive positions.[54]

One of the reasons for male opposition was the fear that the prestige of their profession would be adversely affected if women were allowed to enter. Since women were perceived as being less capable, their success in a certain field would be evidence that the profession was not really so demanding. These male apprehensions were not unfounded. For example, when many women began to work as bank cashiers in 1960, an occupation that had hitherto been considered eminently masculine, its status declined.[55]

But it was not only men who rejected women in "manly" occupations; they were rejected by women as well. Many women, convinced that men were better at these endeavors, looked for male doctors, lawyers, or office managers.[56]

From the above it is clear that for long periods in many societies, the fact that only a small minority of women could claim significant accomplishments in various spheres was the result of societal and legal norms, which did not allow or encourage women to study, work, and create.

In order to determine what women's real capabilities are, it would be necessary to change the social climate and accord women freedom of action in every domain. But such conditions did not exist during most periods of history. Women were not allowed to engage in most occupations or pursuits until the 20th century. There were no female artists until the 20th century for the same reason that there were no black or Jewish artists. In previous centuries, women, blacks, and Jews were oppressed groups.

In recent decades, since women have been granted the opportunity to acquire knowledge, education, experience, and expertise in various professions in science and the arts, the creative power that had been suppressed has gradually begun to find expression. Women have made outstanding contributions in varied intellectual and creative spheres.[57] Even if they have not yet done so in large numbers, their accomplishments have been sufficient to refute the argument put forth by Aristotle, Rousseau, Hegel, Freud, and others as to the essential inferiority of women's capabilities.

That only a marginal number of women have reached the top in various fields derives from the fact that, altogether, relatively few women have turned to these pursuits at all. The greater the number of individuals from a particular population group who are active in a particular area and receive fitting compensation, the greater the likelihood that many of them will have outstanding accomplishments to show for it. Thus, if only hundreds of women are literary writers for a short time, the prospect that they will gain prominence and attain impressive accomplishments in that sphere is less than for men, in whose case thousands or tens of thousands have been active in the course of a long period. When women have received full encouragement to participate in some sphere and have also been properly rewarded, their abilities have been conspicuously evident. In the entertainment industry, an industry in which many women have turned, one finds gifted singers, actresses, and dancers who do not fall short of men in their abilities. For over three hundred years, women who succeeded in this industry were just about the only women who achieved economic independence. They hold an important place in society today, as well. Women have been encouraged to participate in the entertainment industry more than other spheres because, there, they could make use of and emphasize their feminine attributes. Indeed, the big advantage of women in entertainment is that, there, professional success contributes to their sexual attractiveness, so that, unlike other women, they are not torn between conflicting aspirations.

While there have been women who overcame the difficulties and achieved professional accomplishments, the impression remains that women, in general, are not creative or innovative in any way. Women's contributions as participants in important research in the exact sciences, for example, have been glossed over and kept in the background. Therefore, the impression persists that the abilities of women in general do not lie in spheres considered "masculine."[58]

Lise Meitner was the first to discover the process of splitting the atom and to calculate the amount of energy that would be released in the process, thus later enabling the development of nuclear reactors and the atom bomb. Nevertheless, in 1945, it was Otto Hahn who received the

Nobel Prize for Chemistry for his contribution to splitting the atom. Lise Meitner was only awarded the American prize and was selected as "Woman of the Year" for her contribution.[59] The same was true for the mathematician Lady Ada Lovelace, inventor of the binary system in the nineteenth century, a system without which a computer could not work, but the historians have neglected to note her contribution.[60]

Women themselves also contributed to the absence of feminine renown when they elected to use pseudonyms. Many other women were to be found behind the pen name "Anonymous." George Eliot and George Sand used masculine names to preserve their anonymity in order to avoid the deprecatory stigma of female artist.[61]

The degree of success enjoyed by women in earlier eras, when they had not yet been banished from spheres of activity outside the home, is not known. Almost no utensils or other objects made from perishable organic materials such as straw baskets and wooden implements – which could have been the work of women – remain in existence. Archeological research has shown that the earliest utensils were not used to hunt large animals but rather to gather vegetables and to hunt small creatures.

Up-to-date anthropological models place women alongside men in shaping human destiny through creative thinking, crediting them with an especially important role in creating language. These models contradict the assumption that in ancient times only men hunted. Considerable evidence exists that in preliterate societies women exhibited considerable knowledge and expertise, even in matters of hunting.[62]

The conception that women are endowed with less professional ability than men is also being challenged. Freud's judgment that women who engaged in preeminently "masculine" areas (surgeons, engineers, judges, factory managers, political party heads or prime ministers) were nothing other than repressed homosexuals, "masculine" females whose nature was warped – can no longer be taken seriously now that women have entered various professional spheres and proven their abilities. Much of what was described by Aristotle, Rousseau, Hegel, and Freud as characteristic of the universal nature of women was actually only characteristic of women at a certain time. These men believed that they were describing the "nature of woman," but, in fact, they only delineated the female image as it appeared to them. In his era, Freud discovered the phenomenon he called "penis envy" among middle-class women in Vienna, and on that he based his theory of femininity. According to that theory, when sexual differences are first perceived, they have a clear value: the girl, becoming aware of the absence of a penis, immediately knows that it is that which she wants.

As a result, she defines herself and her mother as flawed and inferior. But young women are fully aware of men's superiority long before they are exposed to "penis envy," and the jealousy they feel is toward those qualities that the penis symbolizes: strength, status, and reward.

Even assuming that the penis envy which Freud observed in women of his day actually existed, as a man of science, he should have asked why women considered themselves inferior. The answer is to be found in the status a society contemporary assigned to women: Victorian society afforded women many reasons to be jealous of men. It limited women with laws and prohibitions. If a woman was jealous of the freedom, stature, and benefits that were the lot of men, and in the depths of her heart, she aspired to these things, she was, in effect, wishing that she was male. For her, the penis symbolized all the advantages which masculinity bestowed – therefore, "penis envy."[63]

As noted, the general inferiority of women in Victorian society was a result of prohibitions and constraints. But if the woman's abilities are indeed inferior abilities, there is no need to prevent her from acquiring education and a profession with state laws and social sanctions, because she will not succeed in any case. The need for enforcement and coercion was a result of the fact that female inferiority is not inherent and that women are indeed capable of acquiring an education and a profession and excelling.

Since the paucity or absence of female creativity is not due to some mysterious essence but is instead anchored in limitations and prohibitions that have been imposed upon women, the non-creative past does not predict a similar future. The future remains open.

"Women Live for Others"

It is argued that it is the woman with female characteristics who understands the needs of others and concerns herself with satisfying them. The feminine woman is supportive, compassionate, affectionate, and loving.[1]

In order to examine this assertion, let us return to Carol Gilligan's study and the Heinz dilemma. Heinz' wife, it will be recalled, is dying of cancer, and Heinz does not have the $2,000 necessary to buy the medicine that would save her life, the discovery of the village pharmacist.

One of the chief questions which respondents were requested to answer was whether it was permissible for Heinz to steal the medicine from the pharmacist in order to save his wife's life. From the responses Gilligan received, she reached the conclusion that women think and speak in a "different voice" because women care about others significantly more than men do. Gilligan refers to this concern for others as feminine morality, and she demands that it be integrated into political and social ethics.[2] If the "feminine" factor were indeed to be incorporated in political thought, social-political morality would incline in the direction of a socialist, communist, or welfare state regime, based upon the principle of distribution according to need and which abrogate or limit the right to private property.

The female respondents to Gilligan's questionnaire preferred a policy of welfare over respect for the right to private property. But this does not necessarily imply that Gilligan found a fixed way of thinking. An explanation that is not rooted in a conception of the eternal nature of women should have precedence. Such a conception would not exclude women who do not prefer a welfare state and deem them aberrant, whereas the theory which assumes an innate way of thinking does place such women outside of the norm. Also, Gilligan's research is deficient in that it did not encompass a larger group of respondents from different population strata.

Other psychological studies, which examine various population groups, do not support the conception of women as more empathetic or altruistic than men. Observed gender differences on the issue of empathy are not consistent and are generally very small.[3] A study among poor black migrants in the United States who returned to the rural south shows that men and women do not differ significantly in their value judgments; they agree on questions of behavior toward others and express similar attitudes regarding rights, ethics, and the desirable social order. So, even if Gilligan's conclusions were valid for males and females of the middle class, they do not hold for other classes.[4]

Gilligan's study is also limited in that it deals with a theoretical question and does not examine behavior and decisions in practice. Her respondents were not asked to actually sacrifice their own welfare in order to care for another in need. No question in the study asks whether the respondent would be concerned for others at the expense of her/his own needs. Therefore, Gilligan's conclusions do not serve to prove that women are always ready for self-sacrifice. It is known that when the test is a true one, i.e., when concern for the welfare of another is at the expense of concern for oneself and is unrewarded, the picture changes. Psychological studies that have dealt with the question of whether men and women will involve themselves in the problems of others and proffer assistance, have shown that the determining factor is not a "general" ethical attitude, as Gilligan suggests, but that it is rather dependent on circumstances.[5]

Not only does Gilligan's study not necessarily demonstrate that women are ready to sacrifice their own welfare for others; but even when it would seem that women desire the good of others, it is possible that this desire is influenced by their perception of their own potential benefit. It is reasonable to assume that when women support a policy of welfare or expanded state involvement for the good of the needy, they are, in many cases, also thinking of state support for themselves. It is not necessary to assume an innate way of thinking in order to explain women's support of a policy of welfare, because such support can be explained by the circumstances of their own lives and insecurity concerning their ability to support themselves. When a woman with small children is left without the financial support of her husband, or when she reaches old age without an income, she thinks that a welfare state would be beneficial for her. Many women prefer the welfare state because they have not learned to act independently to help themselves, and therefore, they lack faith in their ability to support themselves.

Evidence that many woman's support of a welfare policy stems from the circumstances of their lives rather than from empathy can be found in the fact that approximately 80% of those receiving welfare payments in the urban United States at the end of the 20th century was comprised of women or children supported by women.[6] The fact that women respond with clear expressions of compassion when asked about their moral position concerning the needy can also be explained by the way in which many girls were raised. The claim that altruism is an inherent feminine trait does not give proper weight to the extensive pressures that are exerted on women from childhood to assume a "giving" posture toward those around them. The education of women is entirely geared to make altruistic sacrifice, second nature for them. Women's or young girls' concern for others at the expense of fulfilling their own needs was accepted with satisfaction by the surrounding environment, whereas opposite behavior was accompanied by punishment and criticism. Girls were raised to believe that if they put their own best interests first, they would be considered unfeminine. The woman was expected to put the needs of her family first and to be prepared to sacrifice herself completely for the good of her children. She was taught to define herself in terms of love, which meant complete self-abnegation on her part and unreserved giving to her husband or her children.

These sacrifices for the sake of marriage and love were demanded only of women. Men were not brought up to think that love meant boundless giving. In contrast to women, men were not asked to love so unconditionally that they lost their own identities.

Society made it legitimate for men to focus on themselves and define their abilities and achievements according to their work. The doubts of men focused on the question of "am I a doer?" and not "am I a giver?"[7] Unlike the woman, the man was not compelled to compromise his career, aspirations, inclinations, realization of his potential, the realms of his interests, his hobbies all for the sake of love and marriage.

It is this acquired female behavior, that of self-sacrifice, which was perceived by Freud as "natural masochism." The perception of woman as masochistic by nature is at the root of the view that being attacked by a rapist or being beaten by their husbands is consistent with women's hidden desires. Apparently, this was the cited reason for the relatively light sentences imposed on those who assault women.

The assumption that women are masochistic by nature finds many expressions in male attitudes. In the recent past, rape was a recurring motif in many pornographic movies, which was thought to supposedly arouse women and make them eager for sexual relations. This attitude also provided an excuse for disregarding a woman's resistance to having sexual relations; on the assumption that deep inside the woman wanted to be raped, the rapist is seen as fulfilling her desires.[8] This approach also provided justification for any rude or violent treatment of women.[9]

The argument that women are "masochistic" by nature is also based on the fact that many women remain with husbands who beat them despite the humiliation and continuous suffering. Some see this as confirmation that women surely desire such treatment, because, otherwise, they would leave.

However, female "masochism" can also be explained by the life circumstances of the women who are beaten. The traditional role set for women in the family and society does not encourage them to display anger or to leave but rather to stay and to try to understand and change things. In religious scriptures and even in Rousseau we find that the woman must please her husband. She must fear him and fulfill all his wishes – even when he behaves obnoxiously. The husband is her master and not her friend, and she must obey him as a servant, for otherwise, she will be forced to do so. To criticize battered wives for not changing their situations and rebelling against degrading treatment is tantamount to charging them with doing exactly what society has demanded of them.[10]

Such an argument neglects the fact that women have been economically dependent upon their husbands. When a woman does not possess economic means of her own, she is afraid to leave her husband lest she is not able to support herself and her children. Even when a woman decides to leave her husband, she loses her social approval that being linked to a man provided her with, i.e., society does not respect a woman who lives alone. Her value increases when she is married. Until relatively recently, women were subject to considerable familial and social pressure to marry. Because of this social climate, many women who suffered in their marriages preferred to remain married and tried to compromise. They also did so out of fear that their potential relationships with another man would not be any better.[11]

However, in recent decades, a change has occurred. Current data show that most women no longer stay with men who abuse them. While they sometimes remain in the relationship and attempt to solve their marital problems for a long time, eventually they leave. Most women who leave say that before deciding to do so, they tried to improve their relationship with their husbands for several years, and it was only when these attempts proved fruitless that they left. It is often the women who initiate the break when the situation becomes intolerable. Statistics indicate that 90% of the divorces in the United States are initiated by women. The divorce rate, which reached 50% in the United States at the end of the 20th century, and the "feminization of poverty," show that women today prefer to forsake the family unit rather than endure an impossible situation, even when this entails a drop in their standard of living. This fact is quite surprising, since it contradicts the prevalent view that it is the woman who is abandoned by the man.[12]

The data indicate that women in abusive relationships choose to get divorced. However, some argue that feminine masochism is expressed most conspicuously in the relations of the mother to her children, both through the children's upbringing and in the woman's very willingness to bear them. Freud maintained that the masochistic elements of the mother's psyche found expression in her readiness to suffer for the good of her children. Nature has ensured that a woman's love for her children is stronger than her love of herself.[13]

The fact that the experience of giving birth to children is accompanied by pain does not necessarily lead to the conclusion that women seek pain. The conclusion can also be that they have learned how to bear pain. A woman's desire to give birth in order to become a mother also does not indicate a wish to suffer but rather the desire to undergo an experience that she believes will bring her satisfaction. Motherly devotion, despite the difficulties it entails, is not the same as masochism or self-punishment. If every man or woman who undergoes some painful or dangerous experience that also promises rewards were to be defined as masochistic, then professional soccer players would be included in this category. The young athlete spends hours suffering from cold, mud, and rain, and he anticipates physical injuries. But it is not usual to identify the pain and the injuries that accompany sports activity as the main motive behind the soccer player's choice of career, and he is not considered to be masochistic because of it. But what is considered to be of secondary importance in motivating men is, it would appear, unjustifiably considered primary and pathological when it comes to motivating women.[14]

Even if we were to find that women in all eras had sacrificed themselves for their children, it would not be sufficient to conclude that their self-sacrifice was an innate characteristic. This characteristic can be attributed to social forces and pressures that have been apparent throughout the course of history. In fact, the history of maternal behavior reveals that no universal and inevitable patterns exist; rather, maternal feelings differ in accord with the woman's cultural level and her aspirations, rather than an inherent characteristic. Maternal love is a feeling that may or may not exist, which can be present and can also disappear, can be strong or weak, can single out one child for special treatment or can treat all of them alike. Everything depends on the mother and her life history. There is no consistent maternal behavior that would enable us to speak of an inherent maternal instinct, sense, or approach. When society exerts pressure upon women to maintain relations of selfless giving to their children, mothers often adopt this role in order to avoid criticism or sanctions. When social mores do not explicitly demand this, their behavior is different.

In her book, *The Myth of Motherhood* (*L'amour en Plus*), Elisabeth Badinter describes how, for about two hundred years, the attitude of women toward their children vacillated between indifference and rejection. In urban regions of France during the seventeenth century, one finds alienation and a tendency to abandon children, and these became the norm in the century that followed. At that time, many children died as a result of neglect. During that same period, large numbers of mothers sent their children to wet nurses in the country. It was not unlikely that children would return from these wet nurses disabled, sickly or dying, and many actually died. Village women who had just given birth preferred to nurse city infants for seven francs a month, after they found women poorer than themselves who agreed to nurse their own babies for five francs a month. In any case, the risk of early infant mortality was high. The difficult economic situation of the natural mothers was the reason usually offered to explain the mass exile of city children to wet nurses.

However, this was not always the case. From data that details the death rate of children nursed by wet nurses, broken down according to the occupational distribution of their parents, we find that alongside infants of poor families, there were children of parents who worked together and whose economic situation would have permitted caring for the children with no difficulty. Such mothers could have kept their children at their sides but preferred to work beside their husbands rather than doing what was best for their babies. And there were well-to-do women, unencumbered by economic burdens and also completely free of the influence of traditional values. They had at their disposal all the means necessary to raise their children at home but chose not to do so for hundreds of years. Apparently, they considered child-rearing to be an unprestigious task. Even though well-to-do women were few in numbers, their behavior enables us to assess how natural a phenomenon motherly love really was.

To understand the repugnance that women felt toward motherhood, it should be remembered that in the seventeenth century, society did not take any note or attach any moral importance to the role of a mother. At best, motherhood was regarded as natural, and at worst, common. Women understood that no one would show them appreciation for being loving, sacrificing mothers. The fact that chroniclers during that period paid but scant attention to the subject of motherhood reveals that motherly love at that time was not of special social or moral value. An attitude of neglect, apathy, and lack of interest on the part of the mother was not explicitly censured by the social and moral code until the eighteenth century. Thus, it turns out that the mother, when not subject to social pressure as to how she raises her children, tends to act in accordance with other considerations, and does not necessarily evince love, sacrifice, and responsibility toward the infant she has brought into the world.

The women who refuse to sacrifice their own welfare for the sake of their children are too numerous to allow us to categorize them as pathological deviants, as exceptions who prove the rule.

Therefore, instead of speaking of a motherly instinct, we will focus on the social pressure that emerged in later periods, directed at convincing the woman that both her purpose in life and her happiness were embodied in motherhood alone. However, even with this social message, not all mothers willingly accepted a motherly role involving sacrifice. Many women complain that they have sacrificed a great deal to raise their children, and what they say attests to the degree of disappointment, exhaustion, and renunciation that represents the experience of motherhood to them. Such expressions of discontent on the part of the women who were brought up to be devoted and to make sacrifices are evidence that motherhood is more difficult than most think, and that nature did not bestow upon women enough "instinctive" means to cope with it.[15]

"Women are Motivated by Emotions"

Among the contentions concerning innate differences between how males and females channel their responses and actions is that women respond more emotionally than men. Implicit in this statement is the assumption of female inferiority: to be dominated by emotions means to act irrationally, which limits a woman's ability to participate in public life.[1]

But this argument is not only voiced by opponents of equal rights for women. There are also feminists who agree that feminine values and qualities are essentially different from those of males. However, this does not lead these feminists to conclude that women should be excluded from politics: possessing more developed emotions does not imply that women are inferior. On the contrary, this is the source of women's strength. It is precisely their lack of sensitivity that makes men unsuited for public activity, since such activity demands superior understanding of the world and of people. On this basis, these feminists conclude that women's attributes make them more qualified than men for social and political activities. They believe that love and devotion are morally important in interpersonal relations, and that these values should be central to politics as well.[2]

"Feminine values" and "feminine influence" should be introduced in the political sphere; the importance of feelings should be reassessed, and greater emphasis should be placed on love and sympathy.[3] These feminists believe that science should include "feminine" components as well. Science is essentially masculine, not because the overwhelming majority of those who engage in it are typically male, but rather because the characteristics of science, such as objectivity, for example, are "masculine." Science is cold, hard, impersonal, and objective; women are warm, soft, subjective, emotional.[4]

But the argument that there is an innate male way of thinking that is logical and systematic and an innate female way of thinking which is more emotional is unfounded. Alternative explanations for these differences are preferable.

It is preferable that women are not, by nature, motivated by feelings alone, for if that were the case they would be unable to participate effectively in human life and activities. Similarly, the idea of exchanging intellectual authority and objective science for authority of emotions could be severely detrimental to our lives. Understanding, communication, or cooperation between individuals is not possible when based upon subjective emotions and impulses. In the absence of a common, objective basis for discussion, it is not possible to solve disagreements. How is it possible to choose between my feelings and yours? Dependence upon feelings alone, without intellectual appraisal, is dangerous – even in love, the sphere in which emotion is of greatest importance. In love, emotion is necessary, but it is not the only condition. The mere fact that a woman is attracted to a man does not constitute proof that a connection with him would serve her best interests or that the relationship would not be destructive for her. She must give intellectual consideration to questions of benefit and harm and not follow her emotions blindly to ensure her own well-being. Thus, it is for the woman's well being not to rely solely on her emotions – in love and in any other matter.

Conscious attention is required to examine feelings and emotional control; there is no reason to assume that women are not capable of doing so. There is nothing in their nature to prevent women from assessing their emotions, and when necessary, acting in opposition to them. The many instances in which women followed their feelings can be explained without assuming an essential feminine nature. Throughout history, women depended upon their emotions or intuition (a quick response without intellectual monitoring) for historical, political, and social reasons. They placed the emphasis upon emotions because they lacked education, especially in the areas of science and philosophy, and they lacked the tools for intellectual reflection.

Women were compared to black men and lower-class males who were also considered to be more emotional than white middle-class or upper-class males. Black and lower-class men, deprived of educational and cultural advantage, have been portrayed as childish, naive, unthinking, and natural; they too have been judged unsuitable to fully participate in public life.[5]

The fact that there are many men whose actions are guided by their emotions refutes the argument that there is an inherent difference between all men and women. Lack of education has deprived women of the tools for logical thought and caused them to depend upon their emotions. But contrary to the feminist position presented above, a life based on thwarted educational development should not be encouraged for either women or men. The critique provided by reason and intellect should not be renounced, and feelings should not be our only counsel.

Having demonstrated that there is no inherent emotional difference between men and women, we should also reject the argument regarding the moral and spiritual superiority of women over men. This argument negates the human identity that characterizes members of both sexes, which is in essence the ability to think, examine, confirm, and, when necessary, to make changes.

Additional Determinist Arguments
"Biology Explains the Social Hierarchy"

As we have seen, psychological theories have contributed to keeping women in traditional "feminine" roles in the modern period. But male superiority is also seen in the exact sciences such as biology. The theory of evolution describes the struggle for control as an aspect of natural behavior; it explains that humans gained control over animals because they were superior to them. In nature, the males rule over the females, and in human society men rule over the women. The social hierarchy is justified by biological differences – the natural inferiority of women compared to men.[1] Many of those who argue as such base their conclusions on studies of animals, because, among other considerations, it is easier to conduct laboratory studies on animals. However, male and female animal behavior cannot serve as unequivocal proof of the inherent behavior of women and men. While experiments on animals can be important in many spheres related to the human species, care must be taken in drawing inferences concerning humans. Medical researchers are well aware that it is not enough to merely test new techniques on animals before jumping to apply these techniques on humans; it may be assumed that most socio-biologists would object to the use of a new medicine that had only been tried out on mice, for example.

In any case, male and female animal behavior does not constitute proof of the natural inferiority of human females, because this is not the case in all animal species.

Contrary to the biological contentions cited above, new animal research indicates many instances of female domination, autonomy, and strength; male care of the offspring and cooperation with the female; and monogamous behavior or absence of sexual differentiation among both males and females. From these studies, we learn that the conclusion one reaches when attempting to demonstrate the existence of a "natural" basis for some pattern of behavior may well depend on which group of animals one selects.[2]

Therefore, it emerges that the scientists who sought to ground differences between the human sexes on animal studies were not always acting as men of science whose duty it was to search for impartial truth, but were trying, rather, to justify the existing social hierarchy through their research.

"Women are Less Aggressive than Men"

Even when the studies are conducted on human beings, the weakness of the biological determinism approach stems, among other things, from the way terms are defined. For example, a socio-biologist may not consider the many differences between wrestling in a sports arena and an attempt to compete at crossing a snowfield to be relevant. For the researcher, both might constitute examples of aggressiveness. Aggressiveness, then, would be found in any activity from trading shares in the stock exchange to two people fighting to the death.[3]

Current studies, which define aggression less equivocally, reject the argument that there are inherent differences between the sexes in this regard. It has been shown that aggression is a choice that can be potentially enacted in members of both sexes. A person's level of aggression changes according to the stimulus, as will be seen in the following:

> *I became violent toward the man who left me for a girl-friend – I kicked him and threw him to the ground. I was amazed at my strength during this rage, and my potential for violence given the right provocation.*[4]

These are the words of a woman who violently expressed her anger. But most women refrain from expressing aggression, and because of the many inhibitions produced by social influences, they do not express their anger.[5] Society channels and shapes the way in which its members express aggression. There are societies in which extramarital relations are of no importance, whereas in others, such unfaithfulness results in blood revenge. Women who belong to societies that live by the sword and in which violence is the rule are likely to be more cruel than men in peaceful societies.[6] There are societies in which aggression is not expressed at all, among both men or women. Since male aggression does not exist in all societies, it is not an innate quality but is rather acquired.

The argument that male domination over women stems from inherent differences in aggressiveness and not from social patterns can also be refuted by comparing heterosexual and homosexual couples.

This comparison discloses similarities in power relations between the two types of families. In both instances, power is based on the relative income levels of the partners. This comparative study is of special interest because it reveals the error in ascribing power in the family to sexual characteristics (such as masculinity) rather than social characteristics (such as vocation or income level).[7]

"Hormonal Differences Influence Behavior and Personality"

In the past, it was commonly thought that the ovaries dominated women's personality and that the explanation for any psychological problem could be found there. When a woman was diagnosed with psychological problems, the doctors would prescribe removing her ovaries in order to cure her. After many ovariectomies had been performed, it emerged that the procedure did not have the expected effect on the woman's personality. While symptoms of the cessation of the monthly menstrual cycle are likely to ensue from such an operation, these do not include demonstrable changes of personality.[8]

"Women are Afraid of Success"

In the past, it was customary to link the apparent "fear of success" in women to their physical build. Differences in vocation and higher education were attributed to inherent differences between men and women. But studies contradict this – no link has been found between fear of success and gender.[9]

Fear of success in women can be better explained by the negative social and romantic consequences of that success (men recoil from successful women), rather than as an inherent tendency.

"Women are Less Intelligent than Men"

In the nineteenth century, women were considered less intelligent than men, due to their smaller brain size. But it emerged that the opposite was the case. It is the relation between brain size and body size that is important, and since women's brains are larger relative to their size, the smaller absolute size of women's brains could no longer be used to prove male superiority. Therefore, the matter was quickly dropped.[10]

"Women are Inferior to Men in Their Mathematical Abilities"

In the past, books on psychology would state that although women have a certain advantage in verbalizing, they are inferior to men in mathematics and the sciences in general. While this assertion was correct in the past, the difference between the sexes is narrowing today and even disappearing in tests that examine quantitative ability. The difference between the test score averages of the two sexes, usually between 3-5%, is not significant, and the variance within each sex is infinitely greater than between the sexes.

The negligible difference can be explained by the different expectations for boys and for girls that influenced occupational counseling. It was rare that teachers and counselors encouraged girls to enter educational tracks that demanded mathematical skills.

A further explanation of the difference in mathematical skills is found in the differential spatial experience of the two sexes. Adults with considerable ability to conceptualize spatially, which influences their mathematical ability, have been found in cultures that encourage children to be independent.

When members of both sexes have been accorded independence at an early stage in their lives, they have been shown to possess good spatial and visual abilities.[11]

"Women Tend to Cry"

The fact is that crying has not only been characteristic of female behavior throughout the generations. The tendency of women to cry is explained in large part by the fact that they were brought up to believe that showing their feelings was permitted. More evidence that crying is the result of education can be found in the phenomenon of crying in men such as Benjamin Constant and Diderot, who were in the habit of crying often. Men stopped crying when it ceased to be socially acceptable.

When crying is not considered fashionable and is not encouraged in women either, they too refrain from crying in public.[12] In seventeenth century France, crying, even over the loss of a child, was considered improper; expression of sorrow was permitted only rarely, in cases where some special quality of the dead child justified it. It was not proper to cry over a dead child, perhaps because such expression of grief might be considered to be immodest, or perhaps because sorrow conflicted with the spirit of religion, or else that there was no point in mourning over a child, since he was an incomplete person, just as in our day it is not considered proper for people to cry over their dead pets.[13]

"Women are Interested in 'Feminine' Matters by Nature"

It is argued that women are more interested in their external appearance and household arrangements than they are in other matters. But interest or lack of interest may be explained as ensuing from the social climate and the circumstances of the lives of women and men rather than from inherent characteristics.[14]

Attention to external appearance varies from one society to another and from one era to another. At certain times, men were much more concerned with their appearance than women. In ancient Rome, for example, men dressed in "feminine" style, and in the seventeenth and eighteenth centuries, men would use perfume and wear lace, silk hose, and elegant robes.[15] Until the end of the 20th century, women were more concerned with their apparel than men, since a woman was valued in terms of her beauty, and her clothes played an important part in emphasizing this.

Women's interest in "aesthetics" and home design can also be easily explained by the circumstances of their lives. The men showed almost no interest in their immediate surroundings, since they found an arena of activity and self-expression outside the home. On the other hand, women were confined to the home and so expressed their personalities through the handsome furniture and utensils with which they surrounded themselves. It was women who selected the home furnishings and arranged them according to their own tastes; thus these items, in turn, reflected women's personalities and testified to their taste and talents.[16] The woman spent more time in the home than the man, so it was only natural that she wished her home to be a pleasant and comfortable place in which to live.

"Women Show Less Interest and Initiative in Sexual Matters"

As in all other spheres, women are considered to be passive in the sexual domain. It is said that women possess less sexual desire than men do, and that the latter initiate more sexual relations because, by nature, they are more interested in sex than women; this also explains the tendency of men to develop relations with a large number of women, while women tend to be sexually loyal. A man should not be accused of infidelity, since he cannot resist his natural urges. The woman can remain faithful to one man, because she is not confronted with the same intense temptation as the man. In other words, little thought is given to the possibility that a woman's fidelity is sometimes achieved by means of rigorous self-restraint. Such views are widespread and are used to justify both the sexual aggressiveness of men toward women and the unfaithfulness of husbands towards their wives.

Studies of men who had been sexually aggressive and were then chemically sterilized show that the sterilization was not particularly successful in reducing their aggression; no connection was found between the level of testosterone and aggression. On the other hand, it was found that the social environment, emotional pressure, and physical exertion all influence hormone levels; that is, a high level of testosterone may be the result of behavior rather than the reason for such behavior. Studies of monkeys also demonstrated that a change in social status influenced hormone levels: a change of standing in the hierarchy because of the removal of a dominant member of the group led to a change in the level of testosterone.[17]

Studies also disprove the assertion that monogamy comes naturally to women. It has been demonstrated that the desire for sexual variety is found in women just as it is in men. But it is only in recent decades, when social norms concerning female sexual behavior have become less rigid, that women have expressed this tendency. A comparison of the 1948 Kinsey Report with more recent studies reveals a significant increase in the number of women who are inclined to have sexual relations with more than one partner.[18] Thus, biologically speaking, the sexual drive of women is equal to that of men, but in the past, social conventions and educational traditions caused them to repress their sexual feelings.[19]

The fact that in the past more men than women were interested in having sexual relations is not surprising, considering the commonly accepted definition of such relations. Religion and the law recognized the right of men to have sexual relations with their wives as they saw fit, to have children. The Catholic Church forbade women to use contraceptives, since this would be harmful or damaging to the goal of married life, i.e., bringing children into the world. For this purpose, women's bodies were expected to be at the disposal of their husbands at all times. A similar attitude prevailed in other societies as well, including Japan, China, India, and the Arab world. This concept of sexual relations in marriage allowed the husband to force his wife to have sexual intercourse against her will, if he so desired; there could, by definition, be no "rape" within the framework of marriage. Even today, there are women who are raped by their husbands who believe that they are their masters or have rights over their wives' bodies.

Since women were forbidden to use contraceptives by laws of the state and the church, they were, in effect, denied control over their own bodies.[20] Women's lack of eagerness for sexual relations stemmed from the fact that sex was not considered to be a romantic activity, in the course of which they might expect to reach a climax. Clitoral anatomy was not studied until recent decades; it was not commonly known that women need clitoral stimulation in order to experience orgasm and that, without it, many of them do not reach a climax in the course of sexual intercourse with men. It was known that women masturbate in order to reach clitoral orgasm, usually without vaginal penetration – especially when they do not climax with their sexual partners, but sexual researchers once refused to believe the testimony of women as to how they stimulated themselves. Women were advised to learn to reach orgasm "correctly" as a result of vaginal penetration only. In other words, instead of using the information that had accumulated and concluding from it that this was normal behavior, the researchers decided that women should reach orgasm by vaginal penetration only and that those who did not were physically or emotionally defective. Correctional treatment was supposed to locate the emotional or physical reason for not reaching vaginal orgasm.

In the past, women did not feel free to explain to men exactly what stimulation they needed and to challenge the accepted definition of sex. Men viewed the fact that women do not climax in sexual relations as a given; they did not try to discover what would enable a woman to reach a climax and make that an integral part of sexual relations. For hundreds of years, sex was far from being an enjoyable activity for women. Women initiated sexual relations less than men did, because for women, these relations symbolized male dominance. A woman's role during sexual intercourse, especially in the "missionary" position in which she lies beneath the man and helps him reach orgasm but does not reach it herself, illustrated the inequality of their relationship.

The dynamic that extinguishes love and causes women to be indifferent or uninterested in sex mostly came about as a result of inequality in their relations with men. Many women were surprised that a man could ignore or humiliate them and then expect them to return his love when he wanted to have sexual relations with them. Women instinctively shrank from letting men touch them under such circumstances.[21]

What Remains of the Argument that there are Innate Differences Between the Sexes?

Thus far, we have reviewed and rejected various arguments that claim that women possess certain innate characteristics unique to them. The most sweeping contentions speak not only of particular qualities that are characteristic of women but rather of some innate, feminine "essence." Typical of this approach was Freud's query, "what does the woman want?" which he admitted he found difficult to answer. Implicit in this question is the assumption that there is a hidden feminine essence whose meaning is difficult to decipher. All women are in essence alike, in the way they think and behave, irrespective of the historical period in which they lived, their social position, education, occupation, or marital status.

I shall try to show that not only are the specific characteristics I considered not innate but also that women, like men, do not possess any inborn qualities (way of thinking, behavior, or special desires); when it comes to spheres of knowledge, values, emotions, and behavior, both women and men enter this world in a state of tabula rasa.[1]

Desires and values are not detached from knowledge; but women and men are not born with knowledge and, therefore, they do not possess specific innate desires and values. Because they stem from values, emotions are also not inherent. Since behavior is influenced by knowledge, values, and desires, it too is not innate.

The variety in content of thought and patterns of behavior of women and men and the variation from one society to another and from one era to another in values, desires, spheres of interest, motivation, matters of style, and roles demonstrate that these are not inherent. One does not find universal innate ways of thinking and behaving in neither men nor women. The "nature" of men and of women is exceptionally flexible. If identical twin girls were separated from birth and one were to be raised in a primitive society and the other in an advanced Western society, we would find that their patterns of thinking, their values, and their behavior would be completely different. The example of identical twins separated at birth, as well as the great differences between women and men who live in primitive societies today and their contemporaries who live in Western societies, are evidence that assertions about a "natural" division of roles and behavior according to sex are without foundation.

Almost all anthropological texts cite a number of societies in which the division of roles between men and women is different from the role division in Western society. What is considered to be women's work in one society is often the work of men in another.[2] There are societies in which there is no sexual division of tasks, and every person, of either sex, is expected to perform any type of work. There are societies in which almost every task is defined as either the work of women or of men, with the rigor of the division differing from one time and place to another. In one society, a man who performs a task considered women's work might not encounter any reaction at all; in another society, he might be openly punished; and in a third society, he might earn a sympathetic reaction.

Anthropologists have discovered that in primitive societies today, men, women, and sometimes even children, participate in collective hunting. A study of tribes such as the Agta reveals that there is no division of labor when it comes to finding food, and hunting is not limited to men only. Every member of that tribe, man or woman, can hunt as long as his or her training and ability permit, and he or she stops hunting only when too weak to continue. In these tribes, women do not become hunters only as replacements for absent men, as is the case in other tribes, and they do not hunt only in company with the men but also go hunting independently. These findings suggest a broad model, according to which the woman also hunted in ancient times.

Variation between societies is found with personal characteristics as well. A characteristic considered feminine in one society can be thought of as masculine in another. Attributes that have traditionally been categorized as explicitly feminine such as passivity, a willingness to help one's fellow, and the desire to care for children, characterize men in one tribe, while in another, they are prohibited to most women as well as most men. In the Arapesh tribe, both men and women are "feminine" and "motherly" in character and sexually passive, because they have been brought up to be cooperative, non-aggressive, and to respond to the needs and demands of others, while in the Mundugomor tribe, both men and women are violent, aggressive, and sexually "masculine." Among the Tchambuli it is the woman who is dominant and the man less responsible and more emotionally dependent.[3]

While its influence on shaping the personality and on sexual role differences is very great, society is not omnipotent; one should not fall into the trap of social determinism, that society is able to mold every woman and man as it wishes. Among the women he studied in his research conducted in the late 1930s in the United States, the psychologist Maslow found those who resembled men more than they did other women in their personality and outlook on life. These women exhibited high levels of the characteristics considered by American society to be "masculine" – leadership, strong character, dodging of peripheral matters, courage, and self-assurance.

They refused to confine themselves to homemaking, and strove to combine marriage with pursuit of a career. Even if their salaries were low, these women considered their employment outside the home to be more important than housework.[4] Current studies of differences of behavior and inclinations between the sexes show that most differences are superficial, and that the behavior of men and women is more similar than is usually thought.[5]

Psychologists no longer discern significant differences between boys and girls. An international child psychology conference that took place on July 1979 in Paris was devoted to this subject, and its participants encountered great difficulty in identifying such differences. No proof was adduced to the effect that passivity, a tendency to accept authority, self-denigration, fear, and anxiety are found exclusively in girls. Neither was any evidence provided to imply that the competitive impulse and domination are necessarily typical of boys.[6] Also, no support has been presented for the notion that women are shallow, shy, passive, dependent, less analytical, easily seduced, non-ambitious, and lack self-respect, or as Freud put it, that they lacked moral maturity.[7] All the fundamental biological arguments which link personality to sex have been refuted.[8]

Not only do such external characteristics as hairstyle or dress vary from one culture and era to another but also personal characteristics, behavior patterns, and gendered role differences.

It is not possible to consistently and accurately predict personality traits, ways of thinking, behavior, values, abilities, talents, or IQ based on gender. In the absence of such data as vocational, educational, and cultural background, we would not be able to predict how quickly an individual selected from a group of men or women would run 100 meters, what grade he or she would receive on a math exam, or how he or she would resolve a management controversy based on gender alone. If there are no differences between the sexes in educational and occupational background, there is also no difference concerning value judgments. The few studies that did find such differences also indicated differences in education and in work experience, variables that are significant in determining decisions about values for both genders.

Such differences in value judgment disappear completely when other variables are controlled.[9] Men and women are not born with sexually adapted behavior. Behavior is in the nature of a role acquired by learning. This role is not easily learned. Awareness of the roles that supposedly suit each sex alone does not always suffice to elicit appropriate behavior. That is the reason that experts have often advised parents to actively guide their children toward certain roles. To educate them to fill traditional roles, fathers and mothers were obliged to act differently toward sons than toward daughters, and to meticulously emulate those traits that were considered appropriate for each sex in their own behavior.[10]

If there are no innate cultural or behavioral differences between the sexes, why are so many norms and roles constituted in accordance with gender? One possible explanation is that human beings think in categories to better understand their surroundings. The physical difference between men and women is conspicuous; therefore, differences in behavior and ways of thinking were also mistakenly attributed to it. The dichotomous thinking embedded in this categorization has penetrated into everyday life, and it dictates our dress, our vocations, and our concerns. The first question asked when a new baby is born is, "Is it a boy or a girl?" This lays the groundwork for a division of roles, for orientation in life, and for exposure to suitable expectations and educational influences.[11]

Almost all societies teach the developing female that the distinction between man and woman is relevant in almost all areas of life. For example, in Western society, a girl cannot help but discern that parents, teachers, and friends encourage different behavior depending on gender; toys, clothes, occupations, hobbies, and the division of labor in the family all vary according to sex.

The girl surely notices that, unlike her, boys are not taught housekeeping tasks. She sees that boys are not encouraged to play with dolls, because it would not be suitable or proper (from this also stems the opposition of the boys when they mature to sharing in housework and childcare).

If society is indeed what influences patterns of thinking and behavior via its education system, then patterns of thinking are likely to change once the educational approach is changed. If a small girl is raised with the same demands and rewards, to the same standards of excellence and freedom as her brother, if she participates in the same games and learns the same things, if her mother and father share equally in material and moral responsibility, then we can expect that the girl will behave in accordance with the patterns of an egalitarian world.[12]

The girl will later experience love as a relationship between equals and not as the master/slave relationship that the Hebrew poet Rachel described in her "Woman" (1929):

From down to up...
In this way:
With the devoted and sad glance
Of a slave, of a clever dog.
The moment is pregnant and pure.
Silence
And an unexplained yearning
To kiss the master's hand.

Even if the girl has not received egalitarian education from the very beginning, she can still change herself at a later stage in her life. Some studies dispute the decisive importance of children's earliest years. These studies show that early influences – even if they are important – can be changed and reversed when social circumstances change. In a current study of middle- and lower-class women in the United States and several European countries, it was found that a woman's decision to become a mother is formulated and influenced more by her experience at a later age than by the education she received during her childhood.

Also, there have been women who, despite their traditional upbringing, have changed their perception of the world, and have chosen vocations that were not traditionally feminine, mainly following exposure to different social influences.[13] While the education we receive during our childhood is important, the cultural messages we receive later in life have greater influence.

An unchanging social environment can reinforce personal characteristics acquired at an earlier stage, but new social circumstances can direct the personality into different channels, whether positive or negative.[14]

In his books about the death camps during the Second World War, Bruno Bettelheim demonstrated that the human psyche can undergo rapid transformation when the surrounding environment changes completely: proud people became meek and fearful when imprisoned in the camps.[15] Many researchers have found that women underwent psychological change when their opportunities and options were altered.

When women began to accomplish successful careers in business and the professional world, their self-perception changed as well. They stopped regarding themselves as inferior, felt stronger, and their motivation increased.[16]

Intellectual and philosophical understanding, and not only new social circumstances, can transform perceptions, and as a result, emotional responses and patterns of behavior can change as well.

Through critical thinking, women were able to produce feminist theory and found the feminist movement, without prior changes in the circumstances of their lives. By virtue of their capacity for critical thinking, women can influence society just as they are influenced by it. Women's perception of themselves as victims has some truth in it, but it also contains a denial of their ability to bring about change. If others limit them, then women's resistance to these constraints depends upon themselves. Perhaps it is too much to expect from those whom society has derogated because of their gender, but since women have the ability to understand and to choose, they need not remain helpless victims of circumstances but rather, by challenging the social structure that limits them, they can bring about radical change.[17]

Thus a woman, in her role as mother, can contribute to such a change through the education of her children. In the past, the mother was expected to prepare her daughter for her life as a wife and mother, and she did so, thinking that she was helping her daughter. But with a different understanding of her daughter's needs and welfare, the mother can prepare her daughter for a life in which she can develop more fully, and she can teach her son to treat women respectfully and as equals. If many mothers act in this way, the world can change greatly within a few decades. Even if the surrounding world continues to exhibit hostility to the development of women, mothers can contribute to improving the situation if they provide their children with a critical approach.

In light of what was said, it is not fair to limit women for biological reasons. What has been considered feminine nature is nothing more than the consequence of a system of beliefs and philosophies that may give way to others. This attitude gives us hope for change. It is clear, then, that there is reason to work for the equal participation of women in all aspects of social activities. Since there are no innate differences between men and women in their ways of thinking or patterns of behavior, intellectual capacities, talents, or occupational preferences, there is nothing "natural" about the traditional division of roles between men and women, except bearing and nursing children. Also, there are thus almost no tasks that women with suitable training are incapable of performing by nature, and there is almost no type of work that women do not already engage in, at least in small numbers.[18]

One of the arguments used to justify the traditional division of roles is based on the difference in physical strength between the sexes. There are feminists who believe that the difference is the result of social factors; while women have less developed physical ability, such ability can be cultivated to a considerable degree.

Women who work at bodybuilding, with small breasts and strong stomach muscles, prove just how much the female body can be molded. The female body that has been developed for athletic competition acquires a different form.

Even though women can improve their physical abilities, it would be difficult to achieve complete equality between the sexes in this sphere. The need to prove that it is possible to achieve such equality reflects feminist fears that without it, the theory of equality will collapse, and women will be forced to revert to their traditional roles. But there is no need for women to prove that they are equal to men in physical strength, since in our day it is not of much importance. During periods when people lived by hunting and were obliged to fight wild animals, women's physical weakness may have been significant, but this is not the case in the era of modern technology. Physical strength is no longer as important as intellectual ability, because today most work is mechanized, and many energy applications are activated by the flip of a switch. Thousands of new jobs have been created which are profitable and are suitable for people who excel in intellectual capacity rather than in physical strength. Studies in psychology and the brain show that contrary to what was thought in the past, women have the necessary intellectual capacities to fulfill such tasks.[19]

We have seen that there are no inherent emotional, psychological, or intellectual differences between men and women, and even differences in physical build and ability are no longer material. If so, what remains of the claim that there are innate differences between the sexes? The difference that is still to be considered is that of biological function.

The necessary and sufficient condition for identifying a man or a woman is a specification of his or her sexual organs and their reproductive function. To be a woman means to have a feminine body, female sexual organs, a monthly menstrual period, the ability to become pregnant and give birth, the ability to nurse a child; to be a man means to have a masculine body, male sexual organs, the ability to have an erection, to ejaculate sperm, to impregnate a woman, and thereby father children. These attributes are not open to choice and can only be changed by extreme medical intervention. Aside from these attributes, it is important to emphasize that biological facts do not have to influence thinking, behavior, or way of life.[20]

The fact that a woman can give birth does not oblige her to do so. A woman can choose whether or not to give birth and can decide how many children she wants.

Just as biological facts cannot determine a woman's choices, neither can social circumstances. Different women may respond differently to the same social situation. For example, two daughters can behave differently when it comes to choosing a way of life – one may follow in her housewife-mother's footsteps, while the other can react to her mother's example by choosing to pursue a career. Moreover, the daughter who chooses to emulate her mother may change her mind as a result of acquiring a deeper understanding of women's situation than she had before.

The social environment does not determine behavior, but it does influence it by offering encouragement or imposing sanctions. Both men and women possess the same broad span of ability, but men have been allowed to develop and discover more qualities and abilities than women. The historical inferiority of women was the result of impeding circumstances and not of nature. Some compare women's situation to that of a tree that withers due to difficult and unsuitable climate or unfertile soil. The historical conditions which women have lived under have been harmful to them and prevented their proper, healthy development.[21]

Women and men share a single humanity. Women, like men, have the capacity to think, to choose, and to create; but women have been denied the opportunity of proprerly expressing these faculties. Women suffered from the inferior status that was thrust upon them. Because it was thwarted, their humanity rebelled in a "revolt of nature."

Women's Suffering in Their Traditional Feminine Role

In the United States, in the 1950s and 1960s, the demand that women adopt the traditional "feminine" way of life and be satisfied with their household and maternal roles was at its height in the 19th century. Let us consider briefly what this approach demanded of women.

The psychoanalyst Helen Deutsch, a follower of Freud, believed that women could only retain their femininity if they relinquished any "masculine" aspirations that they had entertained during their adolescence and transferred them to their sons. Deutsch adopts Freud's statement that mothers can transfer aspirations to their sons that they themselves have been forced to suppress: mothers can expect their sons to satisfy everything that still remains of their own masculine complexes. During the same period, many argued that motherhood was the only appropriate way for women to fulfill themselves. The ideal mother was thought to be the one who realized her femininity only through satisfying the needs of the child, who did not look for companionship with broader horizons than that of her children or for additional occupations and interests for her own satisfaction. The woman was to find all her happiness and satisfaction in her children, in her home. She was not supposed to work outside the home or to delegate responsibility for the care of her children to others.[1]

This way of life was considered satisfying and healthy for women's psyche only, since the spiritual needs and the conditions essential for the happiness of men were categorized differently.

The psychologist Maslow divided human needs into five basic categories, arranged hierarchically:

* Physiological needs (food, water, shelter, sex)
* The need for security (ability to predict, order, defense against bodily harm)
* The need for intimacy (belonging, friendship, relations with spouse and children)
* The need for respect (self-respect, recognition, and respect from others)
* The need for self-realization (giving expression to abilities, realizing potential)

These five categories define the conditions for achieving happiness. According to Maslow, when these conditions exist, external conditions cannot deter a person from his search for happiness.[2]

Among those who are in agreement with this approach is the philosopher Joseph Raz. As Raz sees it, a successful life is one of achievement, overcoming obstacles, the use of intelligence, talents, and good judgment in managing affairs, establishing warm and trusting relations with family and friends, zestful and enthusiastic involvement with other people, and long-lasting companionship. An unsuccessful life would be one of complete passivity, when others feed and clean one, and a person is content to remain as he is. Raz thinks that such a life is not even worthy of being called living, that it would be a deformation of human life – lacking action and objectives, a "negative" life because of its unrealized potential.[3]

In the United States in the 1950s and 1960s, the passive existence described above was closer to what was considered suitable for a healthy woman. At that time, the woman was not expected to make use of her faculties; failure to realize her human potential was not considered pathological but rather normative femininity.[4] The girl was brought up to fulfill herself by living through her husband and her son, and that is the way most American women lived during the 1950s and 1960s of the previous century. By the end of the 1950s, the average age of marriage decreased to 18 and continued downward. The relationship between women with higher education and men also began to change. Young women left their college studies in order to marry or because they were afraid that too much education would harm their prospects for marriage. Never had so many women tried to give birth to so many children within such a short span of time. The kitchen became the center of the home, and women learned to sew at home. Women no longer left their homes except to shop, drive their children, or participate in a social event with their husbands. Girls grew up without ever having worked outside their homes.[5]

Since women had been told that men prefer them to be less knowledgeable and capable, and since this was not always the case, women had to pretend, when in male company, that they were less than they really were. Books of advice about how to be a complete woman recommended the following: if you have large dimensions, are tall or strong, you must conceal these attributes so that men see you as small and fragile; it doesn't matter how large you are, you can appear to be fragile to men if you adopt certain habits: stop radiating strength, ability, talent, courage, and instead try to demonstrate dependent behavior so that men will want to protect you. If you are efficient and capable in "masculine" spheres, you must hide it. Indeed, mothers taught their daughters to let men win, to exhibit dependence; it would make the woman more desirable and lessen the chances that the man would leave her if she appeared to be helpless.[6] The woman learned to pretend when she was in male company, because she believed that she would not be accepted as she really was.

Women made great efforts to make the man feel that he was in charge. Women avoided direct speech, steering the conversation, disagreeing with men, or expressing their own opinions in male company.[7] At that time, a woman could not be strong or clever without being harmed as a consequence.

The traditional life cost women dearly in terms of their emotional and physical health. The fact is that the percentage of women who suffered from mental illness was larger than that of men only when the women served in their traditional roles within the framework of marriage. The extent of mental illness among women who never married, widows, and divorcees was similar to that among men in similar circumstances.[8]

Other phenomena that are worthy of noting are the unprecedented degree of emotional collapse and suicide among women in their twenties and thirties; the feeling of despair after forty, when they had finished their roles as mothers; suicides during their forties and fifties; alcoholism (at that time in the United States there were one million reported alcoholic housewives); drug addiction, obesity, and illness that led housewives to monopolize doctors' visiting hours; problems of sexual frigidity and indiscriminate sexual relations; post-natal depression, lack of interest and boredom, despair, and identity problems, even among women who loved their families and their homes; excess sleep and weariness, even when the housework was not difficult and when the children spent most of their daylight hours at school. In most cases, the doctors found no organic illness in mothers who were constantly tired.

This pattern of fatigue and despair recurred among many mothers, but women's issues were not discussed in the media, literature, or in scientific journals for over fifteen years. On the contrary, the message repeated over and over to women was that they must seek self-realization within their roles as wives and mothers and nothing more. They were destined to a fate of "femininity."

Public awareness that women had a problem first surfaced in the midst of this period when, in 1956, one of the magazines published an article concerning a mother who fled from her home. To the editors' surprise, this article aroused tremendous interest, more than any other topic. Suddenly it was discovered that the women who fulfilled only the role of mother and housewife were thoroughly miserable. A magazine article titled: "Why Young Mothers Feel Trapped?" was published in 1960, and the editors invited young mothers with similar problems to write about them in detail. The editors were amazed to discover that 24,000 women responded.

These reactions caused Betty Friedan to conclude that this could not be the result of coincidence but rather a deeply rooted defect in the women's way of life.[9] The problem lay in women's conceptions of happiness and self-realization. Women believed that happiness and mental health could be achieved by living through others and that feminine normality, maturity, self-realization, and identity were not identical to human identity but rather were limited to motherhood and homemaking for women.

According to Betty Friedan, the housewife's job resembled that of the president of a company who not only decides on company policy and prepares comprehensive plans but also devotes most of his time and energy to activities such as cleaning the factory floors and oiling the machinery. The basic decisions concerning raising the children, interior decoration, menu planning, budgeting, education, and leisure activity all demand intelligence. The real satisfaction from "creating a home," the personal relationships with her husband and children, the culture, warmth, security, and tranquility with which the woman invests her home all stem from her personality and not from the cleaning tasks which she performs with her own hands.[10]

Friedan said that most of the housework that takes most of a housewife's time can be done satisfactorily by an eight-year-old child. Several decades ago, institutions sheltering mentally retarded people found that housework was especially suitable to the capabilities of their residents. In many cities, young women in institutions for the mentally disabled were in great demand for housework, and at that time, such work was more difficult than it is today.[11]

One U.S. Department of Labor survey classifying occupations according to the complexity of the skills needed put housework and care of the family on the same level as a parking lot attendant.[12]

According to Friedan, cleaning work, running a vacuum cleaner or a dishwasher, cooking, laundry, etc. did not demand intellectual effort, strong character, or initiative, and therefore they did not enable a woman to develop. A housewife could barely realize her abilities as a woman of average intelligence. An entire lifetime of housework did not even exploit the abilities of a woman of below average intelligence. Boredom and frustration arise naturally in women of average I.Q. who do only housework. These problems did not evolve because too much was demanded of women but rather the opposite, too little.[13] Simone de Beauvoir observed that it was impossible to turn cooking or shopping day after day into something exciting or to exhibit unending enthusiasm for newly polished furniture. Housework as a career was tiring, monotonous, empty.[14]

There are women who are offended by the idea that their work as homemakers requires only a small part of their human potential. But the life of a housewife should not be glorified nor its reality embellished. The important question to ask is whether it is true that housework is not the most creative or demanding activity or, alternatively, whether it requires more than meets the eye from those who perform it.

In 1953, the sociologist Mirra Komarovsky reported firsthand evidence of one day in the life of a typical American housewife:

> *I get up at 6 A.M. and put up coffee and cereal for breakfast and go down to the basement to put clothes into the washing machine. When I come up I dress Teddy (1«) and put him in his chair. Then I dress Jim (3«) and serve breakfast to him and to my husband and feed Teddy.*

> *While my husband looks after the children I go down to get the clothes out of the machine and hang them on the line. Then I come up and have my own breakfast after my husband leaves. From then on the day is as follows: breakfast dishes, clean up kitchen. Make beds, clean the apartment. Wipe up bathroom and kitchen floor. Get lunch vegetables ready and put potatoes on to bake for lunch. Dress both children in outdoor clothes. Do my food shopping and stay out with children until 12. Return and undress children, wash them up for lunch, feed Teddy and put him to nap. Make own lunch, wash dishes, straighten up kitchen. Put Jim to rest. Between 1 and 2:30 depending on the day of the week, ironing, thorough cleaning of one room, weekend cooking and baking etc.; 3 P.M. give children juice or milk, put outdoor clothes on. Out to park; 4:30*

back. Give children their baths. Prepare their supper and help put them to bed. Make dinner for husband and myself. After dinner, dishes and cleaning up. After 8 P.M. often more ironing, especially on the days when I cleaned in the afternoon. There is mending to be done; 9 P.M. fall asleep in the living room over a newspaper or listening to the sound of the radio; 10 P.M. have a snack of something with my husband and go to bed.

I read this account to my husband and he said that it sounded too peaceful, that the children seem to keep out of the way too much. I haven't conveyed to you all the strain of being constantly with the children for twelve hours a day, day in day out.

I wouldn't call myself a contented housewife. I find it hard to be so tied down... I have sometimes the feeling of being imprisoned.

Besides, I find my life dull. I described my day to you. It isn't just one day – it is every day. Believe me there is not enough stimulation in the incessant dishwashing, picking up, ironing, folding diapers, dressing and un-dressing the kids, making beds day in and day out. My social life with the other mothers on the park benches is depressing. I cannot get them away from the same old talk. They have nothing fresh to give me because

> *they, too, are up to their necks in the same routine... I think there must be something wrong with this setup.*[15]

The chronic fatigue of many housewives is the result of their routine work, their monotonous lives, and the lack of stimulation. To the extent that their intelligence is greater than the demands of what they do, the greater their boredom and emotional fatigue. Charles Murray observes that there is a direct relationship between a person's abilities and the difficulty of the challenge he faces. When the average chess player competes against someone on his own level or slightly better (i.e., someone whom he or she can defeat only with great effort), he/she will be completely absorbed in the game. On the other hand, if one's competence is greater than the challenge, the result is boredom. If the abilities are much greater than the challenge (when the game is viewed from the perspective of Bobby Fisher, for example), great frustration ensues, because the person is prevented from utilizing his/her skill and ability.[16]

The absence of challenges and worthwhile experiences chips away slowly at emotional vitality and can lead to despair and the loss of interest in life, especially when it is clear that the situation is not likely to change. Even though women were promised that they would be happy in their domestic roles because such activity suited their nature, housewives were not happy. On the contrary, many women in the United States during the 1950s and 1960s gradually lost the will to live; and when they could no longer bear their condition, they suffered emotional collapse. Medicine and psychotherapy in that period did not successfully solve the problems of women, because they sought the source of the problem within the women themselves and not in social circumstances and constraints or the inappropriate social structure.

This social structure was based on a mistaken perception of the nature of women. The drama of her life stemmed from the conflict between being a free person, able to make choices, to think, and to set goals, and her actual place in society that made her faculties and qualities irrelevant. Women were denied a life of choice and responsibility because they were not offered any alternative to homemaking. Nonconformance to the conventional laws and norms was no alternative, since its price was confinement, social ostracism, or severe censure. A uniform life was prescribed for all women everywhere, and that is the reason that many of them felt a lack of identity.

The way of life that was imposed on women ignored their abilities and needs and failed to recognize that the conditions necessary for women's existence and mental health were identical to those for men. Particularly damaging to women was their renunciation of commitment to a career. At their best, human qualities find expression in pursuit of a career that demands constant development of the intellect, knowledge, proficiency, and creativity. Women who live through others cannot put their abilities to the test. Such a life is devoid of pride and self-esteem, for these are earned by proving one's ability to cope with challenges, by talent and accomplishment.

Women's self-confidence did indeed suffer as a result of renouncing a career. When their children left home and their household obligations decreased, they lacked the self-confidence required to make a change in their lives. In their later years, women who had never worked in their lives encountered difficulty in taking a serious interest in any sphere of activity, and as we have noted, they lacked the necessary confidence to go out to work. By foregoing acquisition of knowledge and a profession for many long years, women hurt their chances of beginning a satisfying new life at a later date.[17]

It should be remembered that, at most, women spend about fifteen years caring for small children, out of a lifetime of about eighty years. The idea that a woman is invariably married and occupied with caring for small children was valid perhaps in the past, when most men and women lived to the age of thirty or forty at most; today, this perception is no longer relevant. Thus, obliging the woman to focus solely upon household tasks for her entire life, sentences her to long years of emptiness and boredom and leads to misery and despair when she does not know what to do with her free time.

Confined to household tasks, women learned to cultivate their external appearance. But when their identity and self-esteem were based primarily on their beautiful appearance, the transition to old age became more difficult and problematic. The age of forty, which is a wonderful age for men, because at this stage of their lives they have gained honor and esteem for their professional accomplishments, is thought to be "the beginning of the end" for women.[18]

Today's culture features two standards of masculine beauty – that of the youth and that of the mature man. A man does not grieve too much when he loses his youthful countenance. Even then, he can be thought of as handsome – heavier, sturdier. In contrast, women's reputation takes a sharp downward turn when they are still in the middle of their lives, since society views them as old only because they no longer look very young. The ideal of feminine beauty was and still is the beauty of youth. It is hard to find middle-aged women in the media, in news ads, in advertising posters, in entertainment performances, or in fashion shows.[19]

The absence of other criteria for women's self-esteem increased the need for relationships with men. The traditional woman was expected to gain her identity and her self-esteem from the man and from her relations with him. She was taught that, without a man, a woman has no value. But just as excessive dependence upon beauty was not good for her, neither was dependence upon a man. Since she had no resources of her own for self-esteem except her relations with the man, ending a relationship with a man was liable to be disastrous for her. A professional career can be a source of support for a woman when her marriage breaks up. In a time of crisis, the working woman does not lose her identity and her self-esteem, because she does not depend exclusively for these upon her relationship with a man.[20]

The problem of a woman who tries to adapt herself to the traditional feminine ideal is not confined to the psychological dimension. Often her ability to survive is adversely affected because of her complete dependence on a man as her source of livelihood. In other words, a life of dependence not only withholds professional training and meaningful job experience from the woman but also entails the forfeiture of economic independence. The husband may turn out to be a broken reed, if he abandons the woman, loses his job or his business, becomes ill or unable to work for a shorter or longer period of time or can no longer work at all, or when he dies. Dependence upon the husband can prove to be especially destructive when a relationship becomes unbearable due to drunkenness, drugs, violence, or infidelity.

A woman who finds herself in such a situation may want to leave her husband but often will not dare to do so because of her economic dependence. A woman left without means of support who joins the workforce without specific professional training and without previous experience will find it difficult to ensure her livelihood. If she is lucky and finds work, the job rating will probably be low, with low pay, and little prospect for advancement.[21]

Woman's traditional education has a debilitating effect in that it teaches her to refrain from expressing anger or reacting to insult or abuse. A woman was expected to exhibit a pleasant disposition and to avoid expressing feelings of outrage, even when they were justified. She was to be loving and giving, compassionate and understanding, no matter what happened. She was to wait until someone fought her battles, since she herself was not supposed to fight back or even to think in such terms.

Rather than coming out against the man who treated her unfairly, the woman looks inwards to explain the man's behavior. She accuses herself of not being good enough; if she were better, her husband would not treat her so. The woman who refrains from expressing her anger openly and continues to show understanding and love no matter what the circumstances acts to her own detriment. Because she does nothing, she invites the continuation of her oppression. The man learns that despite the way he treats her, he can count on the woman's obedience, and therefore he has no reason to change his ways.

Women who openly resist humiliating treatment sometimes succeed in changing their situation, whereas women who keep silent, even when treated unfairly, remain miserable.

The woman whose self-confidence is impaired by economic dependence will not dare to demand that her husband treat her fairly. She has no bargaining chips vis-à-vis her husband so long as she must remain with him because she is unable to earn a living on her own. Only economic independence will enable the woman to weigh alternatives more easily: should she try to improve the relations that are causing her distress, or leave home.

Feminists argue that the huge investment made by many women in repairing or maintaining such relations discourages creative activity on their part, because it diminishes limited energy resources.[22]

Despite all this, there are those who assert that the life of a career woman is no better. Indeed, when, deep down, because of her traditional upbringing, a woman believes that as a mother she must be at the disposal of her children twenty-four hours a day, she is confronted by guilt feelings when she goes out to work. The message she has internalized – that her proper place is in the home – does not allow the career woman to be satisfied. If she wishes to fulfill both roles simultaneously, undivided motherhood and career, she is torn between conflicting desires and cannot live and act as an integrated individual.

The data disprove the argument that having a career is not good for a woman. It has been found that women with stronger commitment to their careers feel better about themselves than housewives do, because the personal reinforcements they derive from their achievements at work afford them a strong feeling of self-esteem and give meaning to their lives.[23] It is found that educated women with careers in the professions or full-time business positions are happier. A 1989 survey of 1,000 working women aged 18-54 in the United States showed that career women were happier in their marriages than women with jobs that were not compatible with their aspirations or who had not received vocational training and whose only occupation was housework.[24] Research also demonstrated that higher education and independence increased the ability of women to enjoy sexual relations, and that divorce was less frequent among educated women.

It was women who realized their aspirations but for whom love and sex were not the guiding force in their lives who reported the highest level of gratification from their sexual relations.

Psychological studies reveal that women with a university education and a professional career exhibit a capacity for full sexual enjoyment far above the average. The Kinsey Reports show that the more educated the woman, the less she tends to sexual frigidity. Contrary to what might be expected according to psychoanalytical theories and the conventional image of femininity, women with a greater sense of self-identity report greater enjoyment of sex and greater ability to commit themselves freely to love and to experience orgasm. Extramarital relations were also less common among educated women and women with careers.

In the United States during the 1960s, it was not unusual for housewives and mothers to pass from one sexual affair to another, with destructive consequences for their marriages. These were intelligent women who felt "incomplete" and turned to sex for satisfaction and fulfillment.

In terms of traditional femininity, if a woman felt "emptiness," the reason must be sexual. So, instead of undertaking a real commitment to work in some sphere of activity, these married women engaged in an unceasing sexual search. They used sex, seemingly, to fill needs that were not sexual, so that even when they experienced sexual orgasm, they felt unsatisfied. The sense of developing their personal identities, of satisfaction and self-realization, which they tried to find in sex, could not be attained through sex alone.[25] Sex cannot constitute a substitute for personal identity, and it alone cannot confer identity on either a woman or a man.

Career women are not only more satisfied with their lives, including their sex lives; they also experience better health and longer life. Studies confirm that for health and longevity, remaining at home can be the worst possible choice for a woman. The following have been found to be the best strategies for extending an individual's life span by a decade or more:

It is desirable that the woman works for pay. Current studies, as well as studies conducted before World War II, demonstrate that women who are employed and receive wages are healthier than unemployed women or women who are not part of the work force. The former suffer less from chronic illness, spend fewer days in bed and less time in the hospital, and require less medical treatment. The most dramatic difference between these two groups of women appears when they grow older. It was found that the women aged 45-64 with the worst health profile were housewives and women who did not seek paid work. The health of unemployed women, those who are looking for work but have not succeeded in finding it, is closer to that of housewives than to that of working women (these findings also apply to men).

It is preferable for the woman to work in a job she likes, which allows her to use her judgment and to be independent. The data refute common beliefs about which types of work cause the most tension. The woman with the highest risk of heart attack is not the executive with the most authority and great responsibility resting on her shoulders but rather the frustrated filing clerk who sits in the back office. Women who have worked at jobs with no future, as sales personnel and clerks and at other jobs with low status, women who do not like their work, women who feel that their superiors oppress them but do not complain about it for fear of being discharged, women who work out of economic necessity and not out of choice – the health risks of them all are distinctly higher than those of women who work by choice.

The best thing a woman can do for her health and longevity is to achieve success and recognition. The mortality rate of outstanding women, mentioned in the 1964-1965 edition of *Who's Who* and who were interviewed afterward over a period of twelve years, was found to be 30% lower than the average for those their age in the population as a whole: prominent female scientists – 30% lower than their contemporaries; senior executive – 26%; educators, including college professors – 36%; museum curators and directors – 54%; female artists and sculptors – 45%; female political leaders – 48%; community service executives – 52%; female doctors and surgeons – 14%; female judges and lawyers – 22%; female architects and designers – 19%. (Identical findings were obtained for men. Men who have an academic education and who are high achievers in vocational, social, and economic spheres live longer.)

Statistical data in the United States also confirm that general satisfaction can serve as a strong tool for predicting longevity and health at a later age. The critical finding is that happiness is important for a woman's health and longevity, whether she works at home or has a paying job. Still, housewives are conclusively less happy and healthy than other women, and they tend to commit suicide more often than women in any other occupation excluding prostitutes.

The belief that combining a career with family responsibility increases the risk of a heart attack is groundless. Women who fulfill many roles, i.e., women who are married and work, either with or without children, are healthier than women in other categories; but this is on condition that the husband is supportive and that the couple maintains an egalitarian relationship. A mother of three or more children younger than school age who works outside of the home will be subject to great pressure with adverse effects on her health if she does not live with a partner with whom she can share the burden; such support is of great importance.[26]

3. Woman and the Other

"The Traditional Woman's Role is Beneficial to Men"

Women's lives are often miserable when they are merely housewives and mothers; but if a woman carries the dual burden of job and housework, and if her husband does not help her and does not approve of her working, her advancement, or her independence, then her life is doubly miserable. For the woman to be able to use her talents in work and also not forego motherhood and a home, it is not enough for a woman who pursues a career in addition to her responsibilities as a mother and at home to take herself seriously, learn, and work; the man must also change his ways of thinking and behaving. For the woman to have a full life, it is essential that there be partnership with her partner, that he respect her as a person and accept her as his equal and share the household chores with her. It would be best if the couple's traditional division of labor were discontinued.

Ideal married life is achieved when neither the man nor the woman interfere with the goals which the other has set for him/herself after serious deliberation; when both the man and the woman pursue their own objectives and help their spouses as best they can to also achieve theirs. Each realizes his/her own aspirations but not at the expense of the other.

There are those who argue that even if it were possible, a world of equality between the sexes is undesirable. If the woman were "like the man" she would no longer be submissive, economically dependent, and passive; if she developed her abilities and became strong, brave, and independent, married life would lose its flavor and love and even the family would cease to exist.[1]

Indeed, there are men who do not want to live with a woman who is strong and independent, intellectual, and has a successful career. There are men who are not ready to play an equal role in the housework and child-rearing. These men want a woman who will sit at home and be inferior to them because only then can they feel superior.

While it is not men who are the enemies of women but rather distorted social principles, a man who advocates such principles harms the woman's chances for a full, satisfying life. A man who looks for a "feminine" woman, threatens her development, her happiness, and even her very being. Alongside such a man, a woman would feel injured, because his conception of her femininity entails her own suffering.

Women's well-being requires that they not plan their lives in the shadow of the psychological deformity of men who do not want a successful woman as a partner for fear that her success will undermine their own sense of superiority. The approach of men who want to prevent women from living full lives of self-realization should be condemned. As Simone de Beauvoir put it, a person can appreciate the beauty of flowers or the charm of "feminine" women, but if these treasures exact a heavy price, they should be relinquished.[2]

It is also important to determine whether these are really "treasures" for men in every way. Would establishing egalitarian relations necessarily be good for the woman and bad for the man? Does the man only benefit from the traditional division of roles?

Contrary to women, men do indeed derive advantages from the traditional way of life. Men are not dependent upon others economically. They enjoy greater power and control within the family. They enjoy professional esteem and a life full of challenge and interest. Men believe that the traditional role division serves their interests: "Yeah, I like being a father. But I must admit that there's absolutely no way I could ever be a full-time mother to them. I couldn't cope with the routine. It's a lot easier to be a father than a mother."[3]

When the issue of equal participation of men in housework and childcare arose in the United States in the 1960s, reservations were voiced. Why should men, who are capable of being statesmen, physicists, or poets, need to wash the dishes or diaper the baby in the evenings or on Saturday mornings, when instead they could be devoting themselves to more important tasks? Very few raised this question in regard to how women lived. No claims were made that women, too, are capable of the same important undertakings as men, and that they have the same need for a more satisfying and interesting life.[4]

Men do not cut their careers short in order to raise the children, but women are expected to do so. One often hears men say that they would prefer that their wives devote themselves to a career only after the children have grown up. Women interrupt their work for many years and lose almost any chance to bridge the gap.

When the woman goes out to work and also fulfills all her traditional tasks, the man's standard of living is improved because of his wife's salary, without any additional effort on his part, while she carries the burden of two jobs. Men's assertion that by nature they do not possess the necessary skills to do housework is of course unfounded; housework is performed today with greater skill by women because they have had more experience. Men who make an effort to do housework will also reach a high level of skill. Recently, we see more and more men with a talent for cooking or with much success in caring for their children. Today, there are some fathers who feed their infants bottles, prepare their food, bathe and diaper them, take them for a walk, hold them in their arms, and get up at night when the baby cries.[5]

As for the advantages derived by men from the traditional division of roles, my findings indicate that the man as well gains when it is not gender that dictates one's pursuits and personality but rather the understanding, inclinations, and talents of each man and woman. Work and personality would be a free expression of the full potential concealed within each person, when he/she is able to choose from among the wide gamut of the domains of human endeavor and when personality is freed from the shackles of sexual stereotypes.

Men too have discovered the advantages that ensue from the discontinuance of the sharp division between the sexes. They concede that although being a traditional, "masculine" man implies security, it also restricts and limits.[6] Some men have expressed a preference for an egalitarian division of tasks: when the woman loves to cook, he washes the dishes; if she doesn't like to clean the house, he cleans it; if he doesn't like to do the laundry, she does it.[7]

Doing housework has its rewards in that men feel less helpless and less detached from their homes. They also gain confidence in their ability to deal with household matters when necessary, if they remained alone. The active participation of fathers in caring for their children also has considerable rewards for them in that it promotes greater closeness with their children.

When woman are equal breadwinners, it benefits men as well. Men often disparage the "parasitic" women whom, they say, do nothing except sit shut away in their homes, while they, the men, fight the war for existence.

The woman depends on the man and makes demands on him, because she is not allowed to lean on herself. The woman asks the man for money and for status, because he possesses these things; only men are permitted to act and succeed. The man can free himself from the burden of the woman's demands by encouraging her to achieve and earn an income on her own; at the same time, the man will be freed of the irksome feeling that he is wanted primarily because of his ability to support her and of the fear that if, for some reason, he is not able to support her in the future, she will leave him. With the traditional division of tasks, a man has good reason to doubt the motives of a woman for joining her lot to his and remaining with him. When a woman is economically dependent upon a man, he may sometimes wonder whether she loves him for himself or because of the support he provides her.

Many men of all ages – married, single, divorced – have come out sharply against women being economically dependent on them, seeing it as women's way of gaining economic security. Many have felt that they cannot trust women: "My wife. All I meant to her was security and an anchor to hold on to. It has to be the biggest turn-off. I want her to want me for myself."[8] When the woman earns an income and is economically independent, the man can be more certain that his marriage exists and is preserved by virtue of the woman's desire to live with him and not for other reasons, particularly the economic one.

A woman's work can enable her to love a man instead of being dependent upon him, to choose a man under less pressure, knowing that her livelihood is secure, and to marry out of love, since she can support herself even without a man at her side. A very difficult problem arises when the husband loses his job or suffers losses in his business if his wife does not work. An additional source of income will lessen the pressures and fears in such instances. The man can even temporarily leave work which does not suit him in order to find something else, to start a new business, to study; he can also allow himself to think in terms of satisfaction from his work and not only in terms of income.

When the woman contributes her share in supporting the family, the man will not need to devote so many hours to his work or to sometimes work at two or more jobs and thus forego enjoyment, hobbies, and other activities. By the end of the 20th century, ninety-seven percent of men with careers also had families, compared with forty percent of the women in top-level positions. But men who work eighteen hours a day cannot have a family life, and they do not have the time to function in the other spheres vital to their happiness and welfare – to develop caring relations with their spouses and their children, to cultivate social relations, and to enjoy indispensable leisure hours.

Opening up the opportunity for women to act within the wider society and contribute their talents to it is likely to improve the general welfare and thus be of benefit to men as well. The more that talented individuals work in some sphere, the greater the chances of finding a solution to problems and of improving what exists. Genius and creative intelligence are rare, but when women, who constitute about 50% of the population, are enabled to work in all spheres, female genius as well will find expression. This means more rapid solutions for those problems that confront humanity in the areas of health, society, politics; it means a contribution to art.

Many advantages will also ensue as a result of the more developed and independent female personality. Relations between spouses within the traditional framework contained many negative feelings: a man who chooses a "feminine," "conservative" woman, one who does not engage in self-development and does not express her abilities, must also take the consequences for this way of life – a bored and boring woman, bitter and vengeful. By the same token that the man cannot demand that his wife give up her work and still not be an economic burden to him, he also cannot expect that she carry out nothing but oppressive household tasks and still not be bored and bitter over her wasted existence.

When interviewed about their wives' going out to work, husbands often stated that, to their surprise, not only did their economic situation improve as a result, but there was also a psychological release – the men ceased to be the only focus in life for their wives and no longer felt guilty for their wives' frustrations with their way of life. According to one of the husbands, not only was the economic burden eased, and it had indeed become lighter, but all of life's demands seemed less arduous ever since his wife had begun to work.[9]

Intelligent men usually welcomed their wives' development and independence, because it added interest and broadened horizons in their relations. Women acquired additional subjects for conversation as a result of their going out to work, and it became less boring to spend time with them.[10]

Women's going to work and their professional advancement contributed to their education and to their involvement in many spheres. They then could also better understand the professional aspect of their husbands' lives. A housewife who was not professionally involved or active usually lacked the background necessary to share her husband's work-related experiences and concerns. She would not manage to join him in working toward objectives he considered much more important than routine daily matters.[11]

Men have often observed that they usually find traditional women to be boring; that they like to meet women on a higher level, women who are their equal in conversation, whom they can respect and love. Men admit that since the advent of the feminist movement, since women have become more independent, it is also more pleasant to be in their company.[12]

Many men have stated that they do not like various qualities associated with "feminine" women, qualities that the traditional way of life has fostered. That life, in which women were dependent upon men both economically and socially, made them the weak link in the relationship and made them hesitant to express their desires, thoughts, and emotions. It caused women to hide their intelligence and abilities, so that men could feel superior. Therefore, when with her husband or in the company of men in general, the woman is not herself, she is wary about all she says and does. Men, who have noticed that women pretend in male company, have commented that they do not like it, that they are tired of seeing strong, capable women pretending they are stupid and helpless.

There have been men who preferred that there not be a sharp distinction between personality traits of men and of women. They appreciated certain qualities in members of both sexes and referred to them as "human" rather than "masculine" or "feminine." Among the desirable qualities, they listed honesty, reliability, common sense, independence, creativity, pride, loyalty, intelligence, friendliness, resourcefulness, self-esteem, sense of humor, wide horizons, open-mindedness, sensitivity, strong character, and amiability.[13]

Blurring the sharp distinction between male and female characteristics can make life more interesting. A rigid division of roles and personal attributes with its inherent predictability is limiting and stifling. Removing inflexible stereotypes makes it possible for individuality to be expressed and makes life more interesting for both sides.

When the woman is able to express her individual qualities and abilities more freely, the man will find that his own situation has improved. A more positive sense of self will contribute to an improvement in the relations between the two. Self-satisfaction and good feelings will be the lot, by and large, of the woman who works and supports herself, who knows that she has accomplished something and is an integral part of the world's doings. Going out to work and developing professionally will contribute significantly to the woman's feelings of fulfillment and self-satisfaction.

While the sense of fulfillment, so different from the emptiness felt by so many housewives, does not come from work alone but rather from a full life in the other important spheres of life as well (marriage, family, social ties), still her career plays an important part in her satisfaction. A woman who works and has a career has a focus for her life. When men stopped treating women like second-class citizens, the anger, bitterness, and frustration felt by women toward men as a result of their inferior status came to an end. Women, now entitled to receive an equal education, to speak in public, to own property, to control their incomes, and to work in the free professions have felt better about their relations within the family.[14]

Some men admit that as a result of the feminist revolution, their relations with their wives have improved: "I think my wife and I have gained a new respect for each other. This was a direct result of my understanding how my expecting her to still be responsible for all the household upkeep, entertaining, etc., in addition to a full-time job was unfair. Since I have begun taking as much responsibility for it myself, and it's hard, I have never done it in my life before, she seems to have opened up to me more, to like me more, and we have more fun together! We're more of a team now than we were." When men no longer decide for women what the women should do and how they should behave, but rather ask them what they want, the women in turn respond more openly and spontaneously than before.[15]

One hundred years of women's struggle for equal rights have discredited the myth that they would use their newly won rights to take vengeful control over men. Ruling over men is not the objective of the feminist movement. Betty Friedan, founder of the movement, has explicitly defined the aspiration of the feminist movement as struggling for women to be considered human beings, no more and no less.

When women proclaim their opposition to being dominated by men, this does not mean that they prefer weak men so that they, the women, can be "strong." One man put it well: "I think they just don't want to be oppressed... I've found in my own life that my woman gets impatient with me when I'm not assertive (and also when I don't take her opinion into consideration, when I'm 'macho')... The important thing is we both say what is on our minds, and both give each other the right to do what we think best."[16]

"Women's Traditional Role Benefits the Children"

During the 1950's and 1960's, it was commonly thought that if the mother did not devote her entire life to her children and if all obstacles to such devotion were not removed, it would cause the children irreparable damage.[1] Later, it was found that factors such as the parents' education, their professions and income level were more accurate predictors of future success during adult life than the amount of time which the mother devoted to caring for her children during the first nine months of their lives. It can be expected that parents with careers will raise children who are more brilliant, independent, and self-assured, children who are less aggressive and repressed, are more likely to have a higher self-esteem, and run less risk of failing in school.[2]

As soon as we stop focusing on the first three years in a child's life and consider the long-range, the example that the mother sets for her children is more important than the number of hours she spent with them as children. Thus, to assess the mother's influence on her children, we need to view her life as a whole.

As adults, men and women are forced to face up to their mothers' sense of wasted opportunities; these people speak of their mothers as heavy burdens they have had to bear. "If my mother had not sacrificed herself so much; if only she had looked after herself!" they say.[3] Children who see much unhappiness and crisis around them find it hard to be happy themselves when they reach adulthood. Many boys and girls grew up in homes in which their mothers were confined to the role of housewife and childcare and who thus lacked fulfillment or self-realization, if they were not actually miserable.

The way in which many men describe their mothers is embedded with anger and sorrow over the fact that their mothers did not ask more out of life. They do not express such feelings when describing their fathers, even though, generally speaking, they did not receive much love from them. Most men did not admire or appreciate their mothers, often described them as "weak," and reproached them for having acquiesced in their inferior status: "He (my father) still does only what he wants, and she (my mother) lets him get away with it. She won't do things or say things which might provoke him, get him angry, or create problems."[4] Many admitted they were aware that their mothers loved them and had sacrificed much for them, but they would have preferred if they had their own personalities, were better educated, and stood up for their own opinions. They were unhappy that their mothers lacked education and were proficient only at doing housework, that they only listened passively to all the members of the family and to the father's complaints and served them all obediently and without complaint, because they believed that was the way a good wife behaved. In retrospect, many would have preferred that their mothers have more opportunity to realize their aspirations. They commented that if they could have changed their mothers, they would have wanted to help them achieve their objectives and to remove the obstacles that blocked their ways; they would have preferred to see their mothers active but not in the traditional ways in which women had been permitted to be active, that is, through their children.[5]

Popular opinion has it that the good of the children demanded the mother's presence at home, because a working woman was under pressure as a result of her many responsibilities and could not be a good mother. But it is clear that even when a mother does not work, she is not more at ease. A twenty-four-hour-a-day mother is frustrated because such total motherhood does not take into consideration her needs as a person. In many cases, the result is frustration, unhappiness, depression, alcoholism, and even emotional breakdown.

Research concerning mental health has found that married women whose only identity is that of a wife and mother are more prone to mental illness than working women, either single or married.[6] When women have help in raising their children, they are more emotionally stable.[7]

A mother who is only a housewife will usually be dissatisfied, because motherhood is not enough in itself to fill a woman's life. Tolstoy's wife gave birth to more than twelve children, and still she always wrote in her diary about the emptiness and uselessness of everything, including herself. Her children were not enough to give meaning to her existence.[8]

Preventing a woman from pursuing a "masculine" career, on the assumption that she lacks the necessary ability, is not consistent with the delicate and serious objective of shaping a human being.[9] It is a mistake to presume that a woman is a good mother by nature and that, from the moment her children are born, she is blessed with an innate motherly instinct, whose guidance is all she needs in order to give her children optimal care.

Simone de Beauvoir asked what role in the whole world demands such refined personal development, such broad perspective, and such deep philosophical understanding as the undervalued task of motherhood. A wise, educated, developed parent is necessary to raise emotionally healthy, well-developed children, who are ready for independent lives. Only a well-balanced and mentally healthy mother, satisfied with her life and her choice of motherhood, who is aware of the responsibility involved in raising a child, can be a "good" mother.[10] Only such a mother can be aware of the responsibility involved in raising a child, and there is nothing natural about such a commitment to motherhood.

Women are better mothers when they feel better about themselves, when they do not experience life through their children, living only for their sakes. When women direct their creativity to additional spheres and enjoy rich lives, they then have the most to impart to their children.[11]

It has been found that working mothers who enjoy their work and who become pregnant by choice are more satisfied with their lives. They are closer to their children and treat them better than mothers who are housewives or mothers who are not satisfied at their place of work.[12] Women who are frustrated and unhappy are not good mothers; they tend to be cold and rejecting which causes their children to be more problematic.[13] It has been found that children whose mothers spend most of her day with them are exposed to many dangers. Often the children are clinging, bored, beaten, guilt-ridden, and feel that they are a burden.

At the height of the era of total motherhood in the United States, the woman's social isolation, the repression of her human potential, and her confinement to the house had repercussions on her relationship with her children. The phenomenon of child abuse was very prevalent among total mothers. To judge by the symptoms discovered in the offices of psychiatrists, social workers, and psychologists, many children during that period were destructive, fearful, and emotionally disturbed, and many infants cried incessantly.

Unusual new problems were found in children whose mothers were always with them, chauffeured them everywhere, and helped them with their homework. Sons and daughters of "full-time mothers" suffered from the inability to bear pain and were irresponsible and unable to set themselves any goals at all. Many of the 1,825,000 men who were rejected for army service in 1940 for neuro-psychiatric reasons were the sons of full-time mothers. This was the origin of the problems of 600,000 soldiers who were discharged for neuro-psychiatric reasons. This was also the disability of almost 3,000,000 men (one fifth of all men in the service) who suffered from psychoneurosis, often only a few days after their induction, because they were immature and were unable to cope with life, live with others, or think and act independently.

These immature boys were the sons of mothers who had devoted too much of their lives to their children, who wanted their children to remain babies, and did not encourage them to grow up for fear their own lives would have no purpose. These women themselves had not acquired the capacities of mature individuals, were not fully developed, and did not think and act independently; their humanity was incomplete.[14]

The well-being of children demands that the mother doesn't have to care for them alone and without help during most hours of the day. There is nothing in the nature of women that makes it essential that care of the children be given over to the mother exclusively, even immediately after birth. Nature requires only that the woman gives birth to the children, if she decides that she wants her own children. Caring for the children after birth can be shared with others, including feeding infants from bottles during the first period of their lives. Not only do children not need their mother's constant attention every minute of the day, such devotion may even prove harmful to them. The intellectual development or social and emotional behavior of the children will not suffer if their mother does not have exclusive responsibility for raising them, as long as the substitute caregivers radiate warmth, attentiveness, and conscientiousness. Daycare centers, too, do not harm children, and spending time in them is not necessarily detrimental to the development of the child. There is no evidence to confirm the assertion that "the worst natural mother is preferable in the long run to the best substitute 'mother' in a daycare center."[15]

Children whose fathers share in responsibility for their care enjoy many advantages. Their welfare does not then depend entirely upon one person. When the mother is ill, absent, too upset, or does not radiate sufficient love and warmth to her children, a loving father can be their salvation. Children of parents who are both deeply involved in their care achieve development test grades above the average for their ages in comparison with children of traditional parents.[16]

The good of the children also demands that there be two sources of discipline. Involvement of the father in raising his children is likely to diminish the anger that many children feel toward their mothers. The mother's control over her children is unparalleled. Even the most loving mother would necessarily seem to be an interdictory authority to her children. In her book *Jealousy*, Nancy Friday observes that even when a mother risks her life for her child, the child will not necessarily be grateful to her for it. All he or she knows is that whenever he or she enjoys him or herself, the mother stops him or her. When both parents care for a child, "blaming Mother" loses its sting.[17]

There is another reason that children benefit if both parents share equal status. Many have commented that while love and affection came only from their mother, she could not be depended upon for anything else. If the father were angry at the children for some reason, their mother did not interfere and did not express her opinion. She was only good for supplying a shoulder to cry on.[18] When the status of the mother is equal to that of the father, it contributes to the welfare of the children in the sense that she can defend them against their father when necessary.

An egalitarian division of roles between the parents, with both also contributing equally to the family income, serves the best interests of the children economically as well. According to the figures from the end of the 20th century, at least 50% of marriages in the United States end in failure. Two thirds of divorced fathers stop supporting their children, so that the full financial burden of caring for the family falls on the mothers. Mothers raise one quarter of all the children in the United States on their own, and also bear the brunt of supporting them, but many women have remained unemployed and devoid of property following their divorces.[19]

From these findings, it is clear that for the good of the children, their mothers should be capable of adequately supporting them. Thus, not only the well-being of the husband but also that of the children cannot be built around sacrifice of the woman's humanity.

The Contribution of Feminism

Most theories of ethics view self-sacrifice as the highest moral virtue of all. This principle demands that the person live for others – put the good of others before his own – as a basic tenet of his life. It is the altruistic person, whose motives are completely unselfish, who is considered a moral person. The intent here is not good will, conviviality, or sympathy, all of which are also found in individuals who act in their own best interests. To be altruistic is to accord preference to the welfare of others over one's own, as the objective of all one's actions.

These theories of ethics equate morality with altruism; only the actions of an individual undertaken for the sake of others is of moral importance. When his actions are selfish, they are considered bad or at least amoral, i.e., morally neutral and not the concern of ethical theories.[1]

It follows that a philosophical theory that equates altruism with morality is of no practical use to those who desire to improve their lives. It does not show a person how to enjoy life and be happy but instead how to sacrifice pleasures and happiness for the sake of others.

In the philosophical literature, it was mankind that was destined to live for others; but in practice, within the traditional way of life, it was the woman who was obliged to sacrifice herself for others. She was required to live and act only for the sake of her husband and children, and often for the sake of the state as well, especially regarding population fertility; she was denied the opportunity of achieving any personal goal whatsoever. She was not seen as someone with her own right to exist but rather as one for whom concern for others was the justification for her existence and was her highest moral duty. Everyone else was more important than she, entitled to her complete devotion.

Women were directly implicated in absolute altruistic morality, whereas men were not expected to make such total sacrifice of their own interests within the family. Therefore, the experience of women provides an important historical lesson, which can prove instructive as to the harmful effect of the doctrine that morality is altruism and that human beings must live only for the sake of others, without at all taking into consideration their own existential needs and welfare. The experience of women demonstrates that happiness cannot be achieved by concern for satisfying the needs of others while ignoring one's own needs and objectives. Self-sacrifice or prolonged self denial and renunciation result in emptiness, boredom, frustration, and even emotional collapse.

In the 1960s, feminists brought the negative consequences of the altruistic theories to public awareness, which had been tested on women. Feminist writings and struggles revealed women's dissatisfaction with the traditional feminine role which had been assigned to them and which obliged them to live altruistic lives. As a result of feminism, women no longer acquiesce in the denial of their right to live for themselves and to choose their own way of life nor do they submit to the demand that they limit themselves to concern for others instead of realizing their own aspirations. At the time, the feminist struggle challenged the perception of motherhood as the highest and most sacred mission of women. Feminists in the 1960s opposed the assessment of everything women did by the criteria of their roles as wives and mothers. Thus, they rejected the validity of such common questions as whether the new activities of women were not likely to interfere with their more important roles as wife and mother. They opposed the attitude that placed the root of the problem in the careers of women, their higher education, taking an interest in political subjects, their intelligence, and individuality. They repudiated the view that saw the aspiration of women for "something more" in their lives as problematic because it might conflict with the roles that are thought fitting and suitable.

The feminists mentioned above came out against the perception that women's every deed and action should be measured against its articulation with their traditional feminine roles. In contrast to the altruism demanded of women, they recommended that every woman ask herself not only what was good for others, her children and husband, but also what was good for her herself. Contrary to the altruistic theory of ethics, they accorded legitimacy to the woman's desire for happiness and demanded recognition of her right to live for herself. Women were called upon to have their own purpose in life that would awaken their creativity and invest them with truly independent identities. This, they were told, could not come about through ordinary work, through punching a time clock, but rather creative activity, a career. Women were also encouraged to take their places in public activities, to participate in making important decisions in government, to influence policy-making.[2]

Feminists at the time called on women to take responsibility for their lives, to choose their own way and thereby influence their futures. They urged women not to conform to the demands made by others that they live traditional lives but rather to oppose the social mores which put them down because of their gender; despite the difficulties, these things were in the domain of their responsibility. Feminists believed that if women were to adopt such behavior, they would acquire influence and would be capable of changing themselves and their surroundings. The determinist perceptions of the nature of women were rejected out of hand. Women were not pawns in the hands of forces beyond their control but rather possessed the ability to change the course of their lives.[3]

The feminist movement at the time made women aware of new truths and came out against traditional attitudes. It explained to women that not only were their personal lives not as they should be, but also that the entire social system, which denied them freedom of action and demanded their sacrifice, was defective. Since women are human beings, they argued, anything that deprives them of their rights as human beings must change.

In order for the woman to be the best possible human being, those feminists believed, women must first change their perception of themselves as inferior, as one fit only for the traditional feminine roles. Men too must change their attitudes and their behavior toward women; they must stop demanding women's sacrifice.

In order to bring about the desired change, it is not enough to change the attitudes of women and men. A suitable political framework that would make this possible and promote it was also necessary.

4. The Political Solution

The Communist State

Altruism in the sense of devoting one's life to others is not an ideal that women and men can adopt in their lives and still flourish. Still, feminists from the radical trend claim that living for others is a cardinal expression of femininity, and hence, this must also serve as the politically decisive and guiding principle.

The political system based on the demand to live for the sake of others, for society as a whole, is socialism or communism. (There is no difference between them except for the means of achieving the goal. Proponents of communism advocate using force to achieve their objective, whereas socialists hope to bring about change via democratic elections.) According to communist doctrine, the life and work of the woman and the man must be dedicated to the good of all; just as in the traditional way of life the service proffered by a woman to others (her children and husband) constituted the justification for her existence, and her "egotism" was rejected morally, so too, according to communist ideology, a woman (like a man) has value only to the extent that she serves the society, whereas her desire to realize her own objectives is proscribed. A woman has no moral right to refuse to live for others; if she attempts to do so, she denies them what is their moral due. Therefore, others have the right to compel her to fulfill her obligations. Social justice, according to communism, demands the use of physical force against any woman or man who does not forego his/her personal objectives for the sake of the common good as defined and decreed by the government.

Advocates of communism believed that the common good would be achieved in this political system, because altruism is in harmony with human nature. In this, their approach is mirrored by that of the radical feminists, who hold that a state administered according to the principle of concern for the other fits the feminine element in human nature. Communist thinkers adhered to a more comprehensive position that declared that a communist state suits human nature in general; they believed that it was possible to carry out policy based on the principle of altruism without destructive ramifications for the freedom and welfare of the people, because both men and women are by nature altruistic.

Radical feminists advocated a socialist-communist state not only because they believed it expressed the feminine element and thus would be good for women to live in; they also believed that the problem of female oppression could be solved more successfully in such a regime than in a capitalist state. A socialist/communist state would do away with the main reason for oppression – private property. In saying this, the radical feminists relied on theories of Marx and Engels who maintained that women's subjugation only stems from economic causes, and that, therefore, the solution is also economic. The two thinkers predicted that emancipation of women would occur in a socialist or communist state in which, along with elimination of private property, there would also be an end to the economic predominance of men and thus an end to their domination altogether. Followers of Marx and Engels urged women to support the communist revolution and promised them that it would bring about the desired equality.[1]

In light of this, one might expect that the phenomenon of discrimination against women would disappear in a communist state that eliminates private ownership. In this state, which, according to the radical feminists, is adapted to the nature of women, women would also enjoy well-being. But the facts about the situation of women in communist countries, as we shall see below, demonstrate that these hopes were not realized. This constitutes a refutation of the argument that the cause of discrimination against women is the private ownership of property and that discrimination would disappear in the wake of the abrogation of such property relations. It emerges that merely establishing a communist state is not enough to put an end to women's deprivation.

The facts also indicate that communist regimes, in which all the means of production were nationalized, did not afford women a better life than have countries that allow private property.

Many communist regimes have collapsed one after another because they failed to offer their citizens a good life. In spite of this, the idea of economic and social equality founded in altruism that they advocated has not withered. Even today, there are those who believe that the ideal itself is exalted and that it was only its practical application that failed. Socialist and communist parties in Western countries still represent themselves as struggling more actively than others for the equality and advancement of women.

Even after the downfall of most of the communist regimes, there are those who persist in their support of the communist option and who may seek its resuscitation, if in some improved version. Therefore, it is worth examining the situation of women in countries in which socialist or communist parties came into power with the principle of equality for women inscribed on their banner. Does the socialist or communist state constitute the best solution for women's issues? It is worth investigating whether it is simply by chance that the situation of women and men in socialist or communist states did not improve or whether this failure was inherent in the nature of the regime.

The first communist party to come to power was in Czarist Russia, later the Soviet Union. Despite the equal rights that were, ostensibly, accorded to women and despite the widespread reports of their realization, the communist revolution, which changed the economic and social structure of the Russian state, did not improve the lot of most women there. The myth of male superiority remained unshaken. In Soviet Russia, almost no women gained entrance to high echelon political office or attained top-ranking management positions. These were the prerogative of men. In the communist party, the true governing body, the percent of women was minimal. Low-level, low-paying jobs and occupations were characteristic of women in the Soviet Union. Although many women there worked at jobs classified in the United States as "masculine," these jobs were of the lowest status and pay; the most difficult and fatiguing physically; and also the dirtiest (98% of the municipal sanitation workers were women).[2] The women were also obliged to bear the double burden of work outside and in the home; they worked, in effect, 80-90 hours per week.[3]

The radical solution according to which men would share responsibility for housework and childcare was never even considered. No public figure ever called upon men to undertake such responsibilities when women worked in the factories or the offices. The closest to any such stand was Lenin's suggestion that men "lend a hand to the women."[4]

The women participating in decision-making centers were too few in number for them to be able to make public figures aware of their problems. Women needed the permission and cooperation of the male government officials who controlled the press if they were going to find a platform for public protest about their dual role and the burden of the responsibilities they were obliged to carry out without help from their husbands; such permission was not forthcoming.[5] Government officials did not allow publication in the nationalized media of outspoken criticism of sexual discrimination at work. They did not permit the founding of a feminist movement as we know it in Western countries, and indeed, no feminist movement arose in a communist state. During the Brezhnev era, several women who protested against the inferior status of women in Soviet society were exiled.[6]

The negative attitude of communist regimes towards feminism in its original sense stemmed from the fear that feminism was liable to upset their subjection of women.

Feminism is not consistent with the spirit of communism because it places too much emphasis on women's right to control their bodies and their fate; feminism insists that the woman is not merely an instrument to be used economically or sexually. The demand that women have control over their bodies and their lives was liable to detract from the power of the government to exploit the procreative and productive capabilities of women for the "common good." This attitude, which regarded women as the means for achieving ends determined by others, found expression in an international conference of women that took place in communist East Berlin. All the reports and working papers presented at this conference, which was conducted by men, set forth the opinion that the value of women inhered in her "carrying future generations in her womb" and her "dual social role as mother and child-bearer." Throughout the entire congress almost no mention was made of the fact that women are first and foremost human beings whose rights derive from their humanity and need no other justification.[7]

This attitude found clear expression in paragraph 122 of the Soviet Constitution of 1936 in which motherhood is described as a social function, i.e., as a specifically feminine capability that must be used for the common good.[8] This capacity was indeed activated for "the common good." The leadership in communist countries dictated to women when they were to bear children or refrain from bearing children, according to the needs considered essential at the time, whether the objective was limiting the population (as in China) or expanding it (as in Romania under President Ceausescu). The fact is that in the Soviet Union this policy fluctuated in accordance with the changing relationship of immediate production needs and population size. Policy concerning abortions thus had its ups and downs according to how essential women were in the work force at the time.[9]

The woman, with her ability to procreate and her ability to work, served as an economic instrument that the government was entitled to use in its own interest. Just as there was a birth policy, so too, the activities in which women could engage altogether were defined by the regime. In communist states, in which all spheres of activities were nationalized, women were unable to avoid decrees from above. In the absence of alternatives (such as private schools), women were forced to acquiesce in their fate when the government decided not to invest resources in professional training for women in certain spheres.

In communist Czechoslovakia, the government openly prevented women from participating in training and study programs in vocational schools, arguing that they had already exceeded their upper quota. In professions in which the percentage of women was high, steps were taken to prevent "feminization" on the grounds, among others, that children need their mothers at home all day and suffer when they are absent.[10]

When the common good is the guiding principle in a country, there is no argument that a woman can attempt to oppose it. The contention that she should have the right to act in her own interests is the antithesis of the moral ideal of the communist state. In other words, a woman cannot advocate communism without simultaneously condoning the abrogation of her freedom that is its logical consequence.

By the same token, she cannot separate communism from its implications for welfare. Some feminists believed that women's situation would be improved if the government were to encourage women to work by, among other things, establishing subsidized daycare centers. Indeed, in the Soviet Union, most women worked, and daycare centers were subsidized. But the centers could care for only one third of the children up to age six. Since it was hard to find place in nurseries, most women did not give birth to a second child. Even when the working mother did manage to find childcare solutions for her children, her life was very difficult. In addition to her work outside the home, she was also responsible for the housework, so she was ready to collapse at the end of the day. (Apparently, the arduous physical effort influenced the life expectancy of women in the Soviet Union. At the beginning of the 20th century, women's life expectancy was two years less than that of men, despite the longer life expectancy of women in other parts of the world; at the beginning of the 1960s, it was eight years less than that of men.[11])

The great fatigue of women can be attributed to two major causes. One was the refusal of the men to help the women with the housework and care of the children; the second factor was the absence of services and products that could have made their lives easier. The Soviet regime failed to deal with these issues during most of its existence.[12] For example, mothers nursed their children because they did not have the option of feeding them from bottles. There was no diaper service, and disposable diapers were not available. Many women still laundered by hand, sometimes using cold water, especially if they lived in old houses without hot running water. In the large cities, small washing machines were to be found, of Soviet make, semi-automatic, but they demanded almost constant attention. Clothes dryers and dishwashers were nowhere to be found in the Soviet Union. Refrigerators were manufactured without freezing compartments or with very small ones, so that there was no room to store prepared foods. In any event, such foods were almost nonexistent, except in a few restaurants. Women were not supplied with sanitary napkins or medicines to relieve gynecological pains. Contraceptives and information about them were also hard to come by. (Five sizes of diaphragms were theoretically available to women, but in practice it was possible to find only two sizes, and these were without cream or jelly and therefore ineffective). The supply of contraceptives was extremely limited, so that women did not even start to use them. Those who tried the locally made pills complained of such serious side effects as problems with the liver and the blood. Soviet condoms were too thick, inhibiting sexual satisfaction, and the men therefore refused to use them. Many couples used the method of coitus interruptus to prevent pregnancy, so it is not surprising that the main way of controlling the birthrate was induced abortion, which became legal in 1955. It is estimated that approximately 5,000,000 abortions were performed yearly in the Soviet Union.

This state of affairs was made possible because a government monopoly does not need to satisfy consumers, whether in medicine or other spheres. Since its purpose is not for profit, its existence does not depend upon selling products or services, and it can ignore the needs of women. Thus, the woman, as consumer as well, was completely at the mercy of the government and was obliged to settle for what they chose to produce for and supply to her. Services and products were generally of low quality and were even worse the farther one went from urban centers, and this was also true of the standard of living. About fifty million women lived in rural areas on the lowest level, in poverty, and under the most difficult conditions.[13]

Supporters of the communist regime hoped it would bring about individual well-being, but its realization necessitated the use of methods that could not coexist with individual liberties. Therefore, individual welfare was not possible. The communist state, with its planned economy, denies women and men the right to choose their own goals and try to actualize them, and it demands a life of renunciation and sacrifice along with self-abnegation. These are not the best means of achieving happiness and progress. For women, the way of life in a communist state was no different from that which had been their traditional lot. Here too, they were denied happiness and welfare; the only difference was that in a communist state everyone, both men and women, was obliged to practice self-denial. In other words, life in a communist state meant the exacerbation of women's problems rather than their resolution. Women were obliged to live a life of self-sacrifice both as housewives and helpmates for the sake of their families and as citizens for the sake of a larger number of individuals, for the "common good." In a communist state, the woman did not find a solution to her problems, but neither did society-at-large profit. Just as a woman's self-sacrifice as mother and wife was not of benefit to her children and husband, so also sacrificing personal objectives for the sake of the "common good" and living according to government dictates did not bring about the desired result – freedom and equality, prosperity, progress, and happiness for all.

The Welfare State

Since the socialist or communist state does not prevent oppression of women and does not promote her well-being, other feminists contend that the best solution would be found in another type of regime – a moderate form of socialism, known today as the welfare state.

The modern welfare state is a democratic form of government whose objective is to ensure that the basic needs of the population are satisfied through economic intervention. According to its proponents, such an intervention will increase the number of those benefiting from wealth and progress and will expand the opportunities for advancement of most of the people.[1] The welfare state aims to support the needy in time of illness or when they are unemployed; to assist the elderly; to accord recognition to trade unions; to guarantee a minimum wage; to aid disadvantaged families by providing subsidized goods and services. In order to ensure the satisfaction of the weaker strata's basic needs, it is the state that provides education, health services, transportation, and electricity. In spheres that are not considered essential, a certain degree of private enterprise and ownership is allowed. To finance its activities, the government taxes income at rates that increase as income rises.

When women demand additional benefits, they must realize that the result will be higher taxes. When women demand free or subsidized daycare centers, they must also recognize the right of the government to levy additional taxes in order to make this possible. It is impossible to maintain a low level of taxation and at the same time sustain widespread welfare programs. These two options cannot both be realized at the same time; they are mutually exclusive.[2]

For a working woman, taxation means that during the time she spent earning the portion of her salary which was taken from her in taxes, she was working to satisfy the needs of others and to achieve objectives which others had set for her, regardless of any decision she might wish to make.[3] She can only actualize the goals she sets for herself once taxes are deducted from her income. The progressive tax, that increases as income grows, thwarts the possibility that a woman might work more intensively for a certain period of time in order to use the additional money to accomplish her personal goals – studies, opening a business, etc. Higher taxation also forces her from accumulating significant savings, preventing her from taking responsibility for her own future. The taxes collected from a woman's salary can be used by the government as it sees fit, without regard for her personal preferences or plans. The more progressive the tax and the more homogenous people's net income is, the less a woman's standard of living will be dependent upon how she performs her work or on her capabilities. For example, if the public buys the products of a businesswoman or an author's books and most of the profit is taken from them in the form of high taxes, then neither their talents nor their efforts or success will be what determines the level of their income but rather the government.

There are feminists and philosophers who advocate that distribution according to need or the division of wealth be applied not only within countries but also between them, i.e., that affluent societies transfer some of their wealth to less-developed societies, receiving nothing from the latter in return.[4]

Distribution according to need depends upon the productivity of the tax-paying individuals, the efforts they expend in their work, their efficiency. Supporters of a welfare state and the international distribution of wealth assume that women and men will continue to invest effort in their work even when taxes on their income are high, and that entrepreneurs and manufacturers will continue to produce even when their profits are drastically reduced, so that there will be products to distribute. They assume that men and women are utterly altruistic and will work to contribute to the welfare of those who are in need, as defined by the government, even when as a result they are denied the use of their income as they see fit to improve their own lives.

If the assumption about human nature as altruistic is fundamentally mistaken, then high taxes might influence the individual's motivation and impair his productivity. It is reasonable to assume that, in that case, income from taxes would decrease, and eventually, the needy strata would be harmed. The assets of wealthy countries would diminish if their citizens had no incentive to invest effort in their work – if they were not permitted to make use of the fruit of their efforts as they chose.

The facts do not support the assumption of human altruism on which the welfare state is based. The majority of human beings cannot be induced to produce willingly without due recompense. The truth is that most individuals are not ready to invest effort without appropriate compensation. When efficient and productive citizens are burdened with heavy taxes and are not allowed to use their salaries as they choose, their efforts and abilities suffer. The result is to cut off the branch on which all are sitting.[5] For example, if those who develop medicines are not compensated for their efforts and labors, they are liable to refrain altogether from making an effort to discover and produce new medicines. In other words, the assumption that only the taxpayer suffers from high taxes, while all others only benefit, is fundamentally false.

The heavy taxes needed to cover expenditures in a welfare state have a detrimental impact on motivation to produce and often lead to tax evasion. As a consequence, the government then has difficulty in mobilizing the resources required for operating extensive welfare services. Today, there is no longer any doubt that welfare states are not able to provide comprehensive welfare services. They collapse under the burden of welfare costs because the sources of finance fall short. An example of this was Sweden, where the marginal tax rate was 80%, and 60% of the gross national product was directed toward financing public expenses, whereas income was insufficient for this. The problem stemmed from the attempt to carry out a broad welfare policy, while the productive sector contributed less to the economy than the total of the benefits distributed.[6]

The Feminists referenced above supported this welfare policy on the assumption that it would be beneficial for needy women with children. What resolved was that women cannot depend too much upon government assistance when they need it, because when there are no resources, there is more of a tendency to cut back on welfare services.

However, despite these reservations, let us consider, for the sake of theoretical discussion, the opposite scenario. Let us imagine a thriving welfare state, with enough resources to meet the needs of all, including women; the latter would have obtained far-reaching benefits, such as free food stamps for the entire family, so that no woman need fear that she and her children would go hungry. Would this indeed be an ideal situation to which women should aspire?

Even if we assume that a woman in distress would receive serious assistance, this would not be enough to constitute true liberation for her; concern for her welfare would merely have passed from one authority to another, from a particular man – her husband, father, or some other male member of the family – to the government; and just as a woman's dependency upon her husband harms her, so would her dependence upon social institutions. By transferring the concern for her livelihood from her husband to the state, she would only exchange one unhealthy adversity for another. In both instances, her economic situation would not depend upon her efforts.

Experience shows that in the long run, government assistance that is accorded to women and men of the deprived classes, ultimately harms and weakens them, because they become accustomed to making demands upon society and do not make an effort to improve their situation in positive and constructive ways. A woman who is perpetually supported by government authorities has no incentive to change her situation. Often individuals change their approach only out of necessity. One may imagine the following dialogue between a woman and a government official:

- Would you prefer to make arrangements for yourself in old age by working and setting aside some of your income for that purpose after examining various insurance and savings programs, or do you want to sit here and look at television?
- I'm tired. What will happen if I don't do it?
- If you don't do it, I suppose that I will need to do it myself.
- If that's the case, then you do it.[7]

By shifting concern for her future to the official, the woman has not resolved her problem but has instead created a new one. Generations of welfare recipients are testament to the fact that welfare payments never relieve distress. If it were a viable solution, we would not have second and third generations needy in many countries. American Indians received extensive assistance from the government, but they were less successful at freeing themselves from their poverty and improving their economic situation than Far Eastern or Jewish immigrants who received less government help.[8]

Economic success depends first and foremost upon behavioral values – on ambition and willingness to work hard and progress by means of thrift and enterprise. Every group that developed these qualities was assured of success without government help, despite all the obstacles and discrimination they may have faced.[9]

Perpetual dependence is deterrence to development of a woman's self-esteem. Self-esteem comes from investing effort in achieving one's objectives. A woman who proves her ability, takes responsibility for her life, and depends upon herself will be proud of herself and her accomplishments. Her self-assurance would not be helped by transferring the responsibility for her existence from her husband to the state, that is, to another external force.

There is nothing in a woman's nature to warrant persisting insecurity as to her ability to earn a living on her own. An adult woman is not helpless, and there is no reason to assume that she must be supported for her entire adult life.

Certain feminists advocate further government intervention for women's benefit and refer to it as "affirmative action": giving preference to women at work, in their studies, etc. This intervention also entails the risk of harming women, because it is indivisible; it is not possible to transfer to the government the right to treat women as a disadvantaged group without also giving it the right to act for the welfare of other population groups who are considered needy. If the government is permitted to decree increased quotas of women for certain jobs, it would also be empowered to give precedence to the advancement of other groups, defined on another occasion as being in greater need than women.

In certain situations, such as growing unemployment, the government could limit the work of women, if they were perceived as secondary breadwinners whose employment was a luxury rather than a vital need. Methods of limiting the work of women could include not giving tax-exempt status to childcare expenses or increasing taxes on the salaries of their spouses; in other words, government tax policy would be used to impose a fine on the working woman in order to cause her to relinquish her place of work. For this reason, a woman, mother to small children, who wants to work, would find herself in a situation in which almost her entire after-tax salary would go to a babysitter or a daycare center to take care of her children. In many instances, she would probably decide, for economic reasons, to refrain from seeking employment.

Welfare states often adopt this policy towards the work of women. The fact that after the Second World War not many American women went out to work was closely connected to government policy at that time; American policymakers in 1945 were not certain that they could provide jobs for soldiers returning from the war. In light of apprehension that the economy would face a deep depression and mass unemployment, the legislation enacted compelled women to leave work so that the jobs would be available for discharged soldiers. This policy had no economic justification, because it was based on incorrect assessments. As it turned out, there was an abundance of employment possibilities after the war, so that there was no need to have sent the women home. But the American government did not foresee this and took swift action to remove women from the work force. One of the ways they did this was to close government child daycare centers. The protests of the women against this step were of no avail. Federal government support of the daycare centers was cut off in March 1946, and at the beginning of 1948 support by the various states stopped completely.

Other legislation in this direction was the Serviceman's Readjustment Act of 1944, known familiarly as the GI Bill. This law granted fourteen million discharged soldiers free studies in institutions of higher learning, a monthly allowance for living expenses (which was increased by 50% for veterans with family dependents), and low-rate mortgages. This legislation awarded a subsidy or a grant of several thousand dollars a year to each household, i.e., to each family consisting of a working husband, a housewife, and one or more children. This law gave priority to men and caused a regression in the situation of women. Thanks to it, many men received a free education and vocational training as well as preference in the labor market (since it gave at least partial support to dependent family members, this legislation also encouraged early marriage and having children at a young age).[10]

Women's work, their careers, their opportunities for higher education, and also the possibility of performing abortions are all liable to be jeopardized in a welfare state, if the government is afraid that they are causing a decrease in the birthrate. Such apprehensions are not hypothetical: a Japanese Ministry of Health report discloses that the average number of children in Japan gradually decreased from 5.1 children per family in 1925 to 1.57 children in 1990. The Japanese Minister of the Treasury at the time the report was published claimed that the low birthrate was due to the fact that Japanese women were busy acquiring an education and did not have time to raise children. Therefore, he argued, a significant change should be instituted on the subject of higher education in Japan. (Experts say that the reasons for the decline in the birthrate are not actually those mentioned but rather the absence of daycare centers and the difficulty of raising children in the small and crowded Japanese homes.)[11]

Until the recent past, in many welfare states, one saw discrimination against women in almost all spheres of activity. Women were almost completely excluded from top positions in government offices; in government television, women were represented in their traditional role; abortion was often illegal; where education was nationalized, the textbooks reflected the traditional division of roles and encouraged different areas of study for boys and for girls.[12] In Israel, for example, a middle school mathematics text uses a mother buying such and such grams of butter; a biology text instructs the student, in masculine gender, to observe the parts of a fish which his mother is preparing for dinner as examples. When the children grow up, it will be difficult to change their attitudes. Even critical thinking on the part of the adult woman will not always free her from all the sexist stereotypes which she absorbed during her childhood and from her guilt feelings for not fulfilling her traditional feminine roles fully and absolutely, when she works outside the home.

Since, in practice, many welfare states discriminate against women, some feminists have called upon women to organize in large pressure groups so that other groups with opposing interests would not turn all legislation in their favor. For example, lobbying for positive discrimination for women in employment may threaten the employment of men, and the latter, in response, may organize an opposing pressure group that would act to return women to their traditional roles.

In a democratic welfare state, women have no assurance as to the kind of policy some future government might adopt, since its decisions would depend upon a majority vote. Women lobbying for concessions for themselves might not win a majority in the elections, which would be detrimental to them. Even if women do constitute 51% of the population, it is not certain that all of them would favor legislation supporting work and advancement for women. Many women, for example religious women, still hold traditional attitudes about their roles. Therefore, even if government officials today are receptive to certain demands of women, tomorrow they are likely to respond to demands of other groups. Thus, if religious circles gain electoral strength, they may promote legislation that returns women to their traditional roles, discontinue the right to abortion, take away the right to vote, change educational content, etc. By its very nature a welfare state cannot guarantee that it will necessarily support women's interests or any other goals, due to possible fluctuations in majority opinion and because the civil rights of women in it are not immune to government intervention. In the absence of inalienable civil rights, women are dependent upon the good will of the government. For its part, the government is subject to the pressures of other groups of electors – young people, religious, unemployed, and various other types of underprivileged. Therefore, women in democratic welfare states cannot be certain that unfavorable legislation will not be passed in the future.

To this possible deterioration in the situation of women should be added the threat posed by the findings of scientists who, studying the differences between the sexes, claim that women are inferior to men. These studies, clothed in a scientific halo, report the inferiority of women compared with men in this or that sphere, and endanger women and their advancement. It is possible that in the future, based on these findings, a government might prevent women from working outside their homes and might decide to stop investing resources in women's professional education and training. When studies claim to prove that women do not possess equal mathematical abilities (without taking into consideration that such differences are marginal), the operative conclusion in the state in which education is the purview of the government may be not to teach mathematics to girls.

Women's employment in positions of responsibility is liable to suffer if the theory that they are not capable of such responsibility for reasons specific to them (pregnancy, menstruation, etc.) receives a favorable hearing. This possibility is not merely hypothetical, since even until recently, "female" hormones and the monthly menstrual cycle are often cited as obstacles to the participation of women in public life. In the past, a former United States Ambassador to the UN, Jean Kirkpatrick, reported that personages in the White House opposed her appointment because of her female "temperament."[13]

The fact is that policymakers in welfare states are often influenced by the findings of scientists. After World War II, the policy of the American government in blocking work for women was greatly influenced by the recommendations of various experts. The latter urged the government to explain to women that it was undesirable for them to engage in law, mathematics, business, industry, or technology. The experts argued that if the women were determined, despite their natural tendencies, to enter these spheres, they should be stopped. Their emotional maladjustment, which had caused them to leave their homes, made them unqualified by their very nature to work in an office; and, worst of all, the interest that they showed in their work distracted them from what should be their primary concern: the home and the children.[14]

American post-war policy was based on the view, supported by these studies among other things that women should sit at home and care for their children. In 1960, at the beginning of the Kennedy era, there was a White House conference on services for working mothers and for children. The main recommendations of the conference were as follows: in order to safeguard the important mother-child relationship, it would be best for infants under three years of age to remain at home except when there were social or economic reasons to entrust them to caregivers outside the home; individual social service supervision and other counseling services should be provided before and during the period when the mother goes out to work, to enable the parents to decide wisely as to whether the woman's employment would contribute to the welfare of the family more than her presence at home.[15]

At that time neither the good of the woman nor her desires or preferences were thought by the experts and the government to be factors which should be taken into consideration. This situation could repeat itself in the future, if the government were convinced that the good of the state, the good of the children, the stability of the family, or woman's nature demanded that the mother devote herself exclusively to the care of her children and not occupy places of work and study, which belonged to men as primary breadwinners.

Studies of sex differences undertaken in the welfare state endanger the advancement of women for the following reason. Private wealth is neutralized in such states by heavy taxation and eventually the government will be the sole source of funds for scientific research. In the absence of private capital, it is the government that would determine what research programs would be supported and who would receive research grants and thus would influence the direction of research.[16] Without resources, women could not conduct studies that would refute the findings which were harmful to them and which were published in the name of science. If women were not allowed to act because research had determined their inferiority in various spheres, a vicious circle would ensue: they could never disprove the conclusions of such research.

It is expected that scientists conduct their work with maximum objectivity. But when it comes to women, scientists have not always lived up to this expectation, and there are data to prove it. Scientists who found a difference in the intelligence levels of men and women were not free of prejudice and an attempt to deflect the study in the desired direction. When they found that females (because they exhibited greater verbal ability) outperformed males in a test that included certain more verbal questions, the researchers decided to change the type of questions so that the overall result would not be unfavorable to males.[17]

Particularly damaging are the studies that attempt to prove that woman are incapable of making any significant contribution after the age 40 or 50. There were even those who claimed that women's brains wither after age 30. These studies are very harmful to women, who at just that time of their lives (age 40-50) are relieved of the burdens of home and parenthood. Prevention of their professional training, university education, and employment would harm the prospects of women of these ages for economic independence.

The government even determines the age or retirement in public service so that, like men, women are obliged to stop working, against their will, at age 60 or 65, even if they are still strong and able. A compulsory retirement age is unfair in this day and age, especially in more developed countries in the West, when many women at age 60 or 65 are in good intellectual and physical shape. The findings show that the capacity for scientific research and creativity continues after 40 or 50. It emerges, for example, that the productivity of historians, philosophers, and other researchers does not decrease with age. It was found that they published 18% of their work in the third decade of their lives; and 20% in the fifth, sixth, and seventh decades. For researchers in the exact sciences and for inventors, productivity was stable until age 80.[18]

Even though it is not certain that a welfare state would act for the good of women, as can be seen from historical facts, let us assume that the government would adopt an explicit policy of intervention for the benefit of women and would set quotas calling for increased acceptance of women for jobs or studies and their promotion to top positions. This policy is, in itself, flawed in that it does not reward effort or ability and thus cannot get the best out of women. If women know that they will be hired or advanced because of their gender and not because of their abilities or efforts, they will not have the incentive to become more efficient or to invest greater effort, just as workers protected by seniority and other privileges lack such motivation. A woman will be weakened if her acceptance or rejection is unconnected to her ability, talents, or efforts, since control is not in her hands. Even if she tries harder and makes an effort to study, to acquire further education, and to improve and become more efficient, she may not win the job or promotion or be accepted for academic studies because of the quotas.

A woman who is accepted for work or studies can feel satisfied with herself if her achievements are judged solely in relation to her abilities and productivity and not according to irrelevant criteria. But with a policy of quotas, she attains her position and her status by the luck of the draw.

The policy of quotas is also liable to impinge on the assessment of a woman's worth by those around her, especially by her colleagues. The suspicion that working women have gained their positions due to positive discrimination raises doubts about their professional abilities and perhaps even results in refraining from use of their services. Indeed, this method of selecting personnel will surely lead to the hiring of women who would not have reached their positions in circumstances of fair competition. Not only would these women be marked as being unprofessional; this stigma would also rub off on others: those who were ill would hesitate to go to a female doctor; workers would ridicule their female supervisors, and students would have reservations about what was said by female lecturers. Every female professional would find herself the object of suspicions that somewhere in the course of attaining her position her gender had been a contributing factor.[19]

The policy of furthering the advancement of women by increasing quotas is not preferable, since it is also basically unfair. The injustice against women ought not be corrected by means of an injustice against men. The great asset of the classic feminist movement was the justice of their struggle that demanded that women be treated as human beings, no more and no less. If women demand more than men, an injustice is perpetrated against the latter, and the righteousness of the struggle of the feminist movement is forfeited. Women's fight for equal rights is justified, but for no more than equal rights.[20]

Since men's control over women did not disappear in communist regimes and persists in many welfare states, there are feminists who propose the rule of women as a solution.[21] This proposition derives from the idea that the government must always be the agent of the economic or other interests of one class or another or of one sex or another, so that the crucial political issue is which class or sex will gain control of the government to achieve the realization of its interests.

This view ignores the possibility that there may be a political system which respects the rights of individuals, both women and men, and which rejects the rule of some individuals over others by means of force.

Utopia – The Free State

No group has experienced suppression and closure of opportunity as compulsive and persistent as those suffered by women. The means may have varied, but the oppression recurred with unfailing regularity across cultures and throughout the generations: women were burned at the stake as "witches" (the Middle Ages); their feet were bound (traditional China); they walked a number of paces behind their husbands (Orthodox Judaism); they were burned alive upon the death of their husbands (India); they are veiled (Muslim states); they are not allowed to drive cars (Saudi Arabia). They have, in effect, been kept under house arrest, fated to live a kind of apartheid, absent from the public scene, not permitted to act or make themselves heard in the outside world until recent decades in Western countries as in all other parts of the world.

The success of feminism in achieving its objectives depended upon the ability of women to criticize attitudes concerning their innate inferiority and to take action to end their oppression: it depended upon their freedom to publicly express their feminist ideas and to attempt to put them into practice.

The right to speak and act freely is a political one, and because this is the case, it is the political framework that must enable it. The history of the suppression of women, which has fluctuated between greater and lesser severity, indicates that women need to live in a state in which neither the government nor any other authority would be allowed to decide for any woman what is the supreme objective of her existence and compel her to live the life that others feel appropriate. Expressed differently, in order to prevent the recurrence of her suppression, the woman must live in a state in which she will enjoy unalienable individual rights and in which there will be a prohibition on the use of force against her by the government or by other individuals who might jeopardize her life, her freedom, her property, and her physical safety.

Legal recognition of the right to life would protect the woman from designs against her life. It should be recalled that in the Middle Ages, midwives were put to death for no good reason, and thousands of women were burned at the stake as "witches"; until not so long ago, widows were burned to death after their husbands' deaths in India, even if they were only fifteen years old; Muslim women who have had relations with a man before their marriage or out of wedlock and even those who have been raped are murdered by family members for the sake of "family honor"; and female infants were slain in communist China and in India.

The right to freedom: women have been forced to obey laws (enacted without their consent, of course) limiting their independence and freedom of expression. Men, who ruled the state and the family, have been able to introduce prohibitions and constraints regarding virtually any aspect of women's activities of which they disapproved with absolute disregard for the women's viewpoint or even for their humanity. Legal recognition of the right of a woman to freedom would ensure that she is not denied an education, professional training, the opportunity to engage in all spheres of activity and work and at all ages. It would guarantee women the freedom of expression that would enable them to express their positions publicly, to counter and refute degrading and humiliating perceptions without fear of punishment or harassment. It would stop the practice of marrying off girls against their will, at times via arrangements made on the day of their birth (as was customary among Bedouin, Turks, etc. until recently), or of selling them into prostitution (as in Thailand).

Regarding the right to property, in the past, women were not allowed private property and possessions of their own and even their salaries were under their husband's jurisdiction. Legal recognition of women's right to property would ensure them the control of their own possessions and would prevent confiscation by the state or transfer to the dominion of the men in the family.

When others are given jurisdiction over the wealth, which is the product of a woman's work, she is compelled to undertake an obligation not of her own choosing, an obligation without recompense. She is prevented from using the fruit of her efforts as she sees fit and from achieving her own objectives. Rather, it is the state that exploits the fruits of the woman's endeavors to further other purposes.

Recognition of the right to private property would also ensure realization of freedom of expression. Denying this freedom to women was made easier when the government had exclusive control of the media, the content of books and movies, etc.

The right to private property would also ensure the woman that government officials could not compel her – via the monopolistic institutions under government control – to bring children into the world when she was not ready for it, by forbidding the sale of contraceptives or by forbidding the dissemination of birth control information, as was the case, for example, in Argentina. (Both these interdictions were introduced by the Argentinean government in 1975 when it set the goal of doubling the population of the state by the end of the twentieth century[1].)

With regard to the right of women to control their bodies and their health, in the past and even today, operations have been performed on women in many countries to remove the clitoris. About 74,000,000 women have been and continue to be victims of this custom. Operations which damage sexual organs of girls and young women were common in at least twenty African states, Oman, the United Arab Emirates, Southern Yemen, and among Muslim inhabitants of Indonesia and Malaysia, southern Egypt, Ethiopia along the Red Sea coast, northern Kenya, northern Nigeria, and Mali. What in the past had been generally termed "female circumcision" actually included three levels of sexual injury beginning with superficial damage to the hood of the clitoris to removal of the entire clitoris – clitoridectomy, and at its most extreme, infibulation, which is a complicated operation which includes removal of the clitoris, removal of central parts of the inner and outer labia, and stitching closed the vaginal opening along its entire length. Due to the poor sanitary conditions under which the operations were performed, there have been many cases of severe physical damage, sometimes causing death, hemorrhage, post-operative shock, fatal tetanus, and other infections.

In Somalia, one of the husband's tasks immediately after the wedding was to perform the "de-infibulation": to open the sealed vagina with a knife. According to tradition, the man must have frequent and prolonged sexual intercourse with his wife for eight days following the wedding in order to create a permanent opening and prevent the scar from closing over. During those eight days, the woman remains in a constant prone position and refrains, as much as possible, from any movement so that the wound will remain open. In different parts of Africa, it was common also to perform a re-infibulation, i.e., to again seal the vagina, when a woman got divorced. There is appalling medical testimony regarding the infectious results of the accumulation of remnants of urine, blood, and other excretions inside the blocked vagina.[2]

Recognition of a woman's right to control her body and her health entails preventing injury to her, not only by criminals or the government but also by society, the community, and the family. It is vital to prevent injury and destruction to her sexual organs; rape or beatings; binding of her feet and its ensuing deformity as in the case of the ancient Chinese custom, performance of ovariectomy as a way of restoring her to good behavior or, as it were, to treat mental disturbance, attempted suicide, or erotic tendencies. Recognition of this right is essential in order to prevent her being denied medicines which could ease childbirth on the grounds that the suffering of women is God's will, as was once common in Western countries; to prevent her being compelled to wear a chastity belt, a source of discomfort and a danger to her health, as was common during the Middle Ages.

The woman's right to control her own body is also relevant to the issue of abortion. With the birth of a child, any harm done to him/her by the parents would be considered a crime, but not beforehand. So long as the fetus remained in the woman's womb, it would constitute part of her body. Legal recognition of a woman's right to control her body would prevent the forbiddance of abortion.

The rights that have been enumerated here are grounded on an assumption of equality between the sexes; they are general rights that are accorded equally to all. The male shall neither rule nor be ruled, and the same is true for the female.

Preservation of the rights of the male to his life, body, freedom, and property would not violate the identical rights of the female. Thus, the man's right to life would not enable him to take the life of a woman; his right to freedom would not permit him to predicate his happiness on the murder, robbery, or subjugation of women, or on any other injury to their rights; his right to his own private property would not allow him to deprive the woman of hers. Similarly, the right of the woman to life, freedom, property, and control over her body does not give her the power to deprive the man of his rights.

The state that will guarantee its citizens, men and women, their unalienable rights over their lives, bodies, freedom, and property shall be termed a "free state." Such a state has never existed in full, neither in the United States nor anywhere else. Even in the nineteenth century, when citizens enjoyed greater freedom, the government still imposed restrictions.

In communist countries, the power of the government was not constrained by individual rights, either in theory or in practice. Neither men nor women in communist countries possessed rights that were immune to government intervention. In democratic welfare states, individuals do not enjoy absolute freedom as well. Also such states may impose heavy taxes on the income of both women and men, nationalize their property, and even conscript young women for several years to perform "service for the needy" (suggestions in line with this last possibility have already been raised but not yet implemented).

In Western countries, which are freer than other countries in the world, some of the essential rights enumerated above are granted to women but not inalienably. Because these states are democratic, the rights of women are not protected against the possibility that the government, whose power to govern comes from the electorate, might curtail them.

What distinguishes a free state from Western countries today is that in it women's rights to freedom and the control of their lives and bodies are inalienable, while the economy is off limits for government intervention and manipulation. The only task of the government in a free country is to defend its citizens against the use of physical force. The government can only employ physical force against those who first initiate its use.

Except for the necessary means for defense and justice, all the property in a free state would be in the private domain. The media, telephone system, postal service, transportation, schools, universities, hospitals, and clinics would all be privately owned and managed.

Government functions in a free state would be cut back to the minimum necessary to defend the individuals, and there would not be extensive political activities impinging on all spheres of life and necessitating a wide-ranging bureaucracy. The result would be neutralization of an important historical difference between men and women – that between oppressors and oppressed; between men in positions of political power and government and women who are subject to their rule and are obliged to obey their dictates.

The free state would allow the woman to run her life as she chose, as long as she did not use force against anyone else. Thus, it is the only political framework that can enable the woman to live as a thinking person, who makes choices and acts in the full sense of these terms. But what such a state can afford the women is only a potential because the maximum that can be done for her in any political framework at all is to establish conditions that would permit her to live as befits a human being, if she so chooses and if she invests the necessary effort.[3]

The argument that in a free state with a free economy the woman could choose her own goals and act to realize them is disputed by Marx and Engels and their feminist followers. According to Marx, exploitation of women, hierarchy, and patriarchy were implicit in a state with a free "capitalistic" economy. Lee Sanders Comer, a British Marxist feminist, emphasizes the classical Marxist criticism of "capitalism" and argued that "capitalism" requires division of labor within the family according to which the male was considered the main or sole breadwinner, whereas the woman was expected to be the housewife and mother, the consumer, and the emotional support of the male and the children.[4]

This critique, according to which the free economy necessitates hierarchy and patriarchy, is mistaken: it is based on a misunderstanding of the essence of political freedom, a failure to distinguish properly between the free state and the welfare state, and an erroneous equation of economic power with political power. In a free state, no one has the right to compel women to obey others – whether in the family, in society, or in the state; women may not be forced into certain occupations or barred from others. Moreover, no one has the right to oblige women to behave in certain ways economically.

In a free state, in which the use of force is prohibited, economic power can be attained only through free choice. A businessman cannot force a woman to buy his products or services; neither can he oblige her to work for him or to accede without question to whatever salary is offered her. A female worker holds her position by mutual agreement. She has the right to resign from her job, to look for work somewhere else and accept a better offer if it presents itself, or to establish her own independent business.[5]

The fact is that economic freedom does not encourage oppression of women. On the contrary, the greater the economic freedom in any country, the greater the ability of women to express their opinions, to take action and to advance. Women have progressed and developed further in countries that afford greater individual freedom; this is also the case for private spheres in which there is greater freedom from government intervention as compared with those subject to more intervention within the same country.

In the United States, which exhibited many characteristics of a free state, women have made more progress than in other countries. Because the government did not control the media there, women were able to express feminist positions without fear of legal sanctions and punishment as a result of their protests. Also, women's professional achievements in the private sector were unprecedented, whereas in areas under government jurisdiction, such as senior government positions, women's accomplishments were more limited. More women made progress and succeeded in the private sector because they were free to initiate the establishment of private independent businesses. During the years 1977-1980 alone, the number of businesses owned by women rose by 33%. As of the end of the 20th century, women owned one quarter of all small businesses – law offices, insurance agencies, computer services, cosmetics shops, boutiques, and restaurants.[6]

For at least one hundred years (during the 19th century and at the beginning of the 20th century), America was freer than it is today. The greater freedom of that period had a positive influence on the personal characteristics of women. American women demonstrated their independence outside the home and were far ahead of their European sisters.[7]

The earliest generations of American men and women were characterized by determination, independence, responsibility, self-assurance and self-control, and courage. The women, who managed farms and plantations alongside their husbands, were not "feminine" and were not treated like European women. At that time, European tourists described American women as less passive, less childish, and less "feminine" than the women in France, Germany, or England.[8]

During that period, America also led in the sphere of higher education for women. In the mid-1930s, females constituted 40% of the students in institutions of higher learning. In Germany, on the other hand, until Hitler came to power, females constituted only 10% of the students; in Sweden, 17%, and in Great Britain, 22%. In short, during the 1930s, American women were well ahead of their European counterparts along the arduous route to political and economic liberation.[9] As we have noted, this situation changed in the United States of the 1940s. Welfare policy was expanding; and the government was taking energetic steps to return the women home, to their traditional roles, in order to free places of work for soldiers returning home from the war.

Another criticism directed at the free economy by some feminists, again, in the footsteps of Marx, is that the world, which is governed by the free market, is without mercy and devoid of "human" values.[10] Marx claimed that pure capitalism should be rejected because it was inappropriate to his vision of love and fraternity.

Erich Fromm also argued that in capitalism, it is the ethics of fairness that is given validity and not that of love. Marx and Fromm believed that the intimacy that exists between two people in love should be transmitted to the general social system as well. To this, a portion of feminists add that the "human" values are the "feminine" values, because it is women who are more compassionate and concerned for the welfare of others. Echoes of this approach can be discerned in Carol Gilligan who, it will be recalled, in terms of the case she presented to women, maintains that those who are in favor of stealing the medicine for purposes of health and those who support distribution according to need and cancellation of the right to private property are endowed with the qualities of love and compassion.

But those who advocate political freedom are not less humane than those who favor distribution according to need; they are rather more far-sighted. In other words, "feeling" in the sense of concern for the welfare of others is not absent from their approach. The difference is that this approach does not focus on a single issue and the short term but rather stems from the understanding that political freedom is the best and most enduring solution for achieving the freedom and welfare of both women and men. Not only does distribution according to need deny women and men their freedom and their right to private property, but it fails to achieve the objective in whose name it is undertaken – concern for the welfare of individuals, especially the poorer. The facts support this assertion: in our day, it can no longer be argued that the demand for distribution according to need in a socialist or communist regime reflects a more human approach since the primary concern of such a regime is the welfare of the masses. The socialist and communist states that ostensibly offered "humane" safeguards against want did not live up to their promises.

On the other hand, in countries in which there has been greater economic freedom, the well-being of the masses has improved, including that of women. The only system that is able to produce and supply abundance is a free economy, because freedom is a necessary condition for prosperity and welfare.

The Americans were the richest nation in the world because they enjoyed the greatest degree of freedom by far. A wide range of consumer goods, from automobiles, air conditioners, and washing machines to vacuum cleaners and disposable diapers, has been available to society at large, not only to the rich. Every ordinary worker could acquire them and with their help improve the quality of his/her life.

Hunger, cold, ignorance, and disease have been conquered in the freer Western countries, but they are liable to recur if these countries were to deprive their citizens of the freedom that they currently enjoy. When the government dictates its legislation on almost every sphere of life and divests its citizens of most of the fruits of their labors, then economic abundance such as food, knowledge, comfort, luxuries, enjoyment, convenient transportation, good communication will disappear as though it had never existed.

The experience of history is an important criterion for distinguishing a political theory capable of providing a vision that can be actualized from a theory whose promise is illusory Utopia. The theory that says that socialism is more humanitarian because it is better for the masses, cannot live up to its promises, and therefore, should be rejected. Advocates of the socialist and communist theory have ignored the evidence of the failure of regimes that were established in its spirit. When the failure of these regimes became apparent to all, the proponents of communism turned to censuring capitalism for its abundance rather than for poverty (as Marx had done). The ideal of freedom in a capitalist state, they argued, is uninspiring and offers only a "full belly"; it interferes on recruiting people for the sake of more exalted and inspiring ideals such as equality and brotherhood. Such sentiments were still found in writings until recently following the collapse of the communist regimes in Eastern Europe:

> *They are dancing in Prague and dancing in Warsaw, Budapest, and East Berlin. Their joy is understandable, and is easy to identify with. This is the end of tyranny, dictatorship, human oppression. The communist nightmare has ended. It is always good to dance when the nightmare recedes. The question is only what good dream is replacing the bad one. And indeed, it is true that the dream of human redemption had become a*

> *nightmare. But it has receded and been supplanted by the most fatuous and stupid dream possible, the American dream which is superficial, petty, egoistic. Ostensibly, the human being stands at its center as the highest value, but in effect, what it says is only: every man for himself. No one matters but me. Ever since the middle of the 19th century, all the good-hearted, the souls and aspirations of mankind have converged in the spirit of socialism, equality, fraternity, and internationalism. This was the most beautiful dream that was ever dreamed. And when you see that the dream of the American housewife in the supermarket has replaced it, you don't know whether to laugh or cry.[11]*

Socialists are bitter about the fact that the ideal of freedom means only a "full belly," only economic well-being. But for a substantial part of the population of the world, plentiful food remains a distant vision, an ideal, and there is no reason to belittle the economic welfare which freedom offers.

Socialists also argue against those who advocate political freedom for not relegating individualism to a position of secondary importance, and they (the socialists) deride women or men who live for themselves. They protest against the fact that in the freer countries of the West, individuals have the opportunity of trying to realize their own dreams and are allowed to give their own selves precedence as far as values are concerned.

But these arguments as well show a gap in the understanding of the essence of political freedom. The argument that the system offers only a "full stomach" is incorrect, especially from the standpoint of the woman, because the free-state offers a woman not only economic freedom (which enables welfare) but also civil liberties. The defense provided to women in such a state vis-à-vis the use of force against them, vis-à-vis any form of oppression whatsoever, has more than economic significance. That defense, not available to women in socialist or communist countries, welfare states, or in any totalitarian framework, is of the greatest importance. From the woman's point of view, the right to freedom, which she would enjoy in a free country, means, above all, her right to defend herself against those who, in their arrogance, seek to decide for her arbitrarily the social roles and way of life that they think suits her. The most serious problem of the woman so far has been that she has never been allowed to set herself at the head of her priorities and run her life as she sees fit. The opportunity to do so would constitute an innovation that is full of promise.

A French woman of the nineteenth century expressed this position very well:

> *For years, I lived only to fulfill a sense of duty, to the point where I didn't even know what I liked anymore. To live for yourself, that must be wonderful.*[12]

Even though no person can contrive a master-plan dictating how women and men should manage their lives and impose it on others by force in the free state, it would be possible to recommend patterns of behavior and objectives (including common goals) which do not entail the use of force. (Is it possible that for the socialists, it is the coercion that is the element that transforms collective programs or visions into something "inspiring"?)

In a free state, it is not possible to force a uniform collective vision on everyone, and this is of utmost importance to women, for the possibility of inflicting such a "vision" on them is also forestalled. To women, it is especially important that religious coercion, which has played a prominent role in their subjugation, would be among the things prohibited in a free state. In the name of religion, women have been constrained by inferior status and roles limiting them to the home and excluding them from activities in other spheres. Apparently, in a free state too, there would be those who would continue to live in the spirit of religious tradition, but they would not have a monopoly on the performance of marriage, divorce, and burial rites and would not be able to impose on others religious customs and practices that offend and humiliate women.

It is possible that in a free state there would continue to be comparative studies of the sexes testifying to the apparent inferiority of women. But these would not have any practical consequences and would not endanger women. Since the government would be prohibited from initiating the use of force, it would not be able to deny women the opportunity of participating in any of the various spheres.

The principle of freedom guarantees women protection against coercion and domination. In addition, it would accord women complete freedom of action, and this is a change full of promise. Thus far, women have lived in a world in which they have not had full opportunity to try their hands in many areas of activity. It is only in recent years that the prohibitions placed upon them have diminished, and they have successfully entered many spheres previously closed to them.

However, the claim that women have the potential for success in all fields of endeavor has not yet actually been proven in practice. The theoretical argument that women's potential for creativity and success does not lag behind that of men must be tested in practice in order to convince everyone of its truth.

When everything is open to women, without legal prohibitions and without limits – aside from the prohibition against doing harm to others – there will undoubtedly be women who will forge a path to new horizons.

When women enjoy success in a wider range of professions, men's attitude towards women will change, as will that of women toward themselves. As an ever-growing number of women prove to have superior ability and talent in areas previously closed to them, the old attitudes, held by both men and women, will by force of circumstances give way to new ones. The past inferiority of women will then be understood to have been the result of prohibitions and constraints rather than of innate characteristics.

In a free state, women will be able to train themselves and try their hands at whatever endeavors they choose, for the first time in history, be it "masculine" or "feminine," and all possibilities would be open to them without legal restrictions. Therefore, only within the framework of such a state can we discover the potential power of women as human beings. Various feminists who believe that women's nature is different from men's also maintain that liberated women would bring about a different female world. But since women's nature is not different from that of men in terms of innate patterns of thinking and behavior, the only logical expectation is that the abilities of both women and men would then find fuller expression in all spheres of thought and action.

The free state would provide the woman with the most favorable conditions for the maximum realization of her abilities as a human being. But if she is to achieve that potential, she must first be aware that a full human life is possible, fitting, desirable, and legitimate for her as well as for others. Armed with this awareness and situated in a free state that permits her to act on it, the woman can effect far-reaching changes in her condition.

By its very nature, the free state would not impose on the woman the perceptions and choices vital to human life at its best. It would furnish the infrastructure of freedom and its defense. For her part, the woman would need to invest effort in both thought and action in order to attain life at its optimum.

It is important for the woman to be aware of her ability to bring about change in her situation by changing her ways of thinking. Even if as a child she had received a traditional upbringing, much depends upon her and could be changed even at a later stage in her life in order to eradicate harmful attitudes. Many women have accomplished such a change in their lives, even though in childhood they had received a very conservative education, which prepared them for the traditional "feminine" roles.

The uprooting of prejudicial attitudes would, among other things, follow upon the change in perception concerning the areas of activities suitable for women. Women must make efforts to extricate themselves from jobs in the "feminine ghetto" and relocate themselves in positions or endeavors having significance, content, and status. Changing women's self-perception from being supported for their entire lives by men will also help to expunge prejudice. It is desirable for women to have an active orientation towards life, to accept full responsibility for their existence, and to reject the commonly accepted traditional attitude that it is the men who must shoulder responsibility.

Perhaps, in a certain sense, it is easier for a woman to be supported economically by her husband and to experience her life through him and through her children. But for the sake of this false security, she must renounce the development and use of her talents, her pride, and her humanity. Statistical data concerning divorce show that by so doing she may jeopardize her future and the future of her children. (As noted, only one third of divorced American men paid child support at the end of the 20th century.[13])

The free economy can encourage women to depend upon themselves alone, to assume responsibility for their own lives, because in time of crisis (divorce, for example), they would not receive support from the state, and no one would be obliged to come to their rescue. Welfare grants are not possible in a free state, because this would entail depriving others of their freedom. Thus, life in such a state will encourage the woman to seek a marriage in which the economic burden and the responsibility for the home and the children are divided between the couple. For the woman to be able to work and support herself with a job/career and at the same time marry and raise children, she must reject linking herself to a man who thinks in traditional terms in advance. Such a relationship might cause her misery and despair and perhaps even endanger her very existence. If, from the start, she chooses a man who reveals enthusiasm for her way of life as a mature and independent woman, she will not need to decide later between marriage and motherhood or a career.

Placing a career at such a high point on the woman's scale of values could be regarded as a materialistic tendency, but only a small number of women can allow themselves to ignore the fact that they must work in order to live. Economic independence alone can enable them to marry for love or to abandon unsatisfactory marriages.

In order to fully explore this theory, we must clarify what it would do to the woman's life in practice; what would enable the woman who lived in a free state to put this vision into effect, to be married and bear children and at the same time cultivate a career?

The free economy, more than other economic systems, can enable a woman to more easily combine a professional career with the home and family. This is facilitated by new products and services and the conditions that the free market can offer.

Many of the tasks in the home that were once men's responsibility such as painting the house, for example, have become professions, and today, they are performed by trained personnel. This is also true of women's jobs such as baking, sewing, and preparing food. The more women regularly go out to work, the higher the increase of the demand for mechanization and professionalism in the tasks and services performed by women at home, and chances are high that the supply will also increase because it will be economically worthwhile. The free economy is structured to be flexible and sensitive to demand, because profits depend on it. Unsuccessful businesses do not receive government assistance. It is the consumers, by buying or not buying, who determine the economic fate of business enterprises, and, therefore, their inclinations and preferences are taken into consideration.

If demand increases for paid services and technological innovations, which would enable the woman to devote herself to her work even when her children are small, the supply is also likely to increase. (Already today, with the help of the computer, the woman can do many things very quickly, such as paying bills and making purchases, without needing to travel far from home.) Also, increased demand for good daycare centers and schools will influence the supply. In most countries in which education is nationalized, no attempt has been made to adjust school hours to the working day.[14] Combining work with motherhood would be made easier in a free state because the schools, all of which would be private, would want to absorb as many students as possible and would compete among themselves. Therefore, they would be more flexible and responsive to the needs of parents, their customers. It would be easier to introduce changes in a private school's hours, because the schools would not need to function according to government rules.

Business owners in a free state are likely to adapt themselves to the needs of the working woman, not only as a consumer but also as an employee, for economic reasons. Thus, for example, it is worthwhile, on long-range considerations, for an employer to be generous in granting maternity leave to a worker who contributes to the success of the business: a woman has two children on average, but she participates in the labor market for more than forty years.

At the end of the 20th century, there were already signs of a shortage of professional personnel in almost all work branches. Large companies in the private sector began changing their policies in order to attract more women and to keep them at work. Firms shifted their focus to women in order to continue to exist and flourish, and to do so, more and more private businesses organized daycare centers on their grounds or participated in the cost of kindergarten tuition. They adopted the practice of offering their male and female workers a choice not only of flexible working hours but also flexible bonuses, and the employees themselves began to decide which of the bonuses offered was best suited to their needs: free kindergarten education, extended vacation, or augmented life insurance. Such bonuses have proved worthwhile for the employers because they have resulted in greater productivity, fewer absences from work, and general employee satisfaction with the work place. On the other hand, there has been no progress in government companies and institutions toward consideration of the special needs of women as mothers.[15]

Thus, the structure of the free state is able to encourage women to take responsibility for their lives and to help them combine work with family life by offering goods and services that facilitate this. But this combination will not occur by itself, without a suitable life plan involving a change in the woman's understanding of her traditional roles. When women attach importance to their professional pursuits, they will succeed in integrating the two roles. There have been women who have fulfilled their obligations to their professional careers along with marriage and motherhood, taking both jobs equally seriously.

There are those who conclude from the fact that previously, 51% of the women did not manage to combine a career with a family that women must choose between the two. But the very same data reveal that 49% of the women do manage to combine motherhood with a career. The more interesting question for those who do not advocate returning women to their homes is how have women managed to do this? What can we learn from the experience of these women about how to succeed in integrating the two spheres?

The years between ages 25-35 are the most important for establishing one's self at work and building a successful career, but these are also the years when one usually starts a family. It has been found that the woman's long-range interest necessitates that she continue to work even when her children are small. Women who withdraw completely from the labor market during those years are liable to find that they can never catch up. When they try to return to work (usually around age forty), it is very difficult if not impossible for them to get back on track. Women who stop working completely often find that they have nowhere to go back to, even in the sphere of their previous activities.[16]

It has been discovered that it is worthwhile for a woman to employ the help necessary for raising her small children in order to avoid quitting her job, even if her salary is not particularly high and covers no more than the cost of childcare and her transportation to work. (The woman's own good requires that the expense of childcare be considered a joint family expense, like the mortgage and heating the home in winter; it should not be set against her income alone.)[17] After a number of years, she will have a position that will enable her to make a significant contribution to the family income, far beyond what she paid earlier for help in caring for the house and children.[18] The decision to remain part of the workforce is a wise economic decision in the long run.

Uninterrupted employment contributes to an employer's willingness to invest in a woman, and thus it is an important component in her professional advancement. Indeed, many private employers discriminate against women, not because they want to block women's advancement but because they don't want to invest in expensive training of female employees who will leave their work or be absent from it for long periods.

For the woman to be able to continue to work while her children are small, it is essential that she free herself of feeling guilty because her children are in a daycare center or are being cared for by someone else. She must not see motherhood as demanding her constant presence in the home. As we have seen, such excess proximity is not healthy, neither for child nor mother, and work combined with parenthood is both possible and desirable.

In order for the woman to benefit from the advantage of bought services, she must rid herself of the traditional meaning attached to "woman," according to which her primary role is to perform all the tasks in the home personally. Those tasks can be performed efficiently and quickly if only they are not used to justify the woman's existence – if she does not see them as the main goal in her life, and if she does not seek maximum perfection in this of all spheres. Men whose occupations demand ability, responsibility, and decisiveness have found that they are able to complete housework in less time than their wives. When women began to see themselves as fulltime homemakers and took upon themselves additional household projects to make use of the time they had at their disposal, those tasks grew ever more numerous. During the 1950s and 1960s, the American woman spent more time doing housework than her mother and grandmother, even though homes were smaller and easier to maintain, and despite the many appliances that had become available. She devoted more time to housekeeping than the busy farm wife did, because the farm wife had many other tasks to perform as well.[19]

If women take their work outside the home seriously and see it as a career, housework will take second place in their lives, just as care of the car and garden or activities in the basement workroom take second place in the life of most men.

The woman will not need to choose between marriage and motherhood, on the one hand, and a career and loneliness, on the other, if she plans her life well and fights against the feelings of guilt. If she concentrates on what is most important and considers housework as a secondary chore which is not the be all and end all of her existence; if she chooses a supportive and understanding spouse; and if the couple agrees to make use of outside help in raising the children and doing the housework, the woman will be able to continue her work while her children are growing up.

For her work to indeed turn into a career with a high income, the woman not only needs to change her priorities in life but also to invest effort in developing her professional qualifications to the best of her ability. The economic structure of a free state encourages the woman to advance and develop at work, since the government would not be allowed to dictate conditions for acceptance at work. Rather, it is the economic interest of the employer that would determine this by obliging him to hire the most capable workers. In a free economy, the government does not support unsuccessful enterprises, so the reason for hiring workers must be economic, i.e., how much a potential worker will contribute to the firm's profitability.

The profit motive will lead the producer of goods and services to engage the best and most qualified workers that can be found on the market, no matter what their sex, race, background, ethnic origin, or religion. There is nothing in the logic of a free economy that can promote the adoption of a criterion not linked to economic success. The decisive qualities are efficiency, proficiency, ability, diligence, initiative, and devotion. Therefore, it would not be worthwhile for an employer to reject a woman just because she was a woman, since if she possessed the necessary attributes, she could contribute much professionally and economically.

As a hired employee in a free state, the woman would be less vulnerable to the arbitrary whim of an employer than in a welfare state, since in a free economy there is incentive for the employer to hire a woman who meets the requirements of the job, and since the considerations must be those of economic success. In this, there is another important advantage for women: they would be hired only because of their qualifications and job performance, so that they would know that they could feel pride in their achievement when they are promoted and their salary is raised. These achievements will also earn them the respect and esteem of their co-workers.

When efficiency and optimal job performance are not the only criteria for hiring employees, the living standard of women as consumers is adversely affected, as are their prospects of combining a career with a family. And indeed, in a welfare state, these are not the only standards for hiring women workers. In the public sector, it is possible to dismiss an employee only if he or she is found guilty of misconduct or wrongdoing or has grossly neglected his responsibilities, because it is not efficiency or ability that determine whether one remains employed or what will be one's salary. In a welfare state, whose economy is controlled to a large degree by the government, worker efficiency is not decisive for the firm's existence in the private sector either, since that is not what enables the business to prosper but rather government benefits. To survive economically in a welfare state, without the possibility of accumulating capital because of heavy taxes, business owners need incentives, grants, loans, concessions, production quotas, preferential status, tax or customs reductions, and subsidies.

Economic survival is difficult for those who do not receive such benefits. Soliciting government authorities for these supports pays off more than does productive economic activity; the businessman finds it more profitable to devote a large part of his efforts to attaining protection from the government than to invest resources aimed at offering the consumer better and cheaper goods and to this end to hire the most efficient and capable female and male workers.[20]

When a firm receives government support, subsidies, or is government-owned, its expenses increase due to inefficiency, but it is not faced with the question of its continued economic existence and the need to make improvements, to become more efficient and save money. Such firms have no motivation to lower costs and to increase productivity, to exploit a maximum of resources, to cut down expenses. Therefore, the goods and services they produce become more expensive. The person who suffers is the female consumer, who, due to the burden of heavy taxes and the lack of cheaper, competing goods and services, finds that her standard of living and her ability to combine work with her household responsibilities are adversely affected. Thus far, women have found it difficult to combine a career with marriage and parenthood in welfare states, because their salaries have not been high enough to hire the necessary help. Many women do not work when their children are small because of the heavy taxation of their salaries, which is used, among other things, to finance those services that are provided "free of charge."

In a welfare state, the woman does receive services such as health or education free of charge or at a subsidized cost, but in actuality, she pays for these services with her taxes. Because these nationalized services require a bureaucratic administration, the woman could receive more for her money if she paid for them directly rather than indirectly through her taxes. In this way, it would not be necessary to pay salaries to many bureaucrats. To illustrate this issue, here is an example from the sphere of education.

Nationalized education is not free. It is financed by the parents through taxes, and it is more expensive. In the absence of competition, there is no incentive for those in the field to lower their expenses and hire the best people. This means that women pay more for education services that are provided by the bureaucrats as consumers than they would for private education whose supply was motivated by the profit incentive.

Still, many believe that public education in a welfare state is preferable to private education in a free economy, because of the fear that many parents, especially those with low incomes, would not be able to pay the cost of educating their children. But this fear is groundless for several reasons. In a free state, the government would not be able to prohibit dissemination of information about contraceptives or their sale, nor could it prohibit abortions. Thus, the overwhelming majority of children who are born would be wanted, and their births would be the result of a positive decisions that had taken into consideration the possibility of providing for their economic needs. Parents would be able to pay for the education of their children, since every working family already pays a considerable sum for education through its taxes, which finance the public schools.

In a free economy, families with lower incomes could pay for private education, because competition would encourage the formulation and preparation of more efficient educational curricula at lower cost (for example, it might be possible to learn to read in half the time it now takes with a corresponding decrease in the price).[21]

A great advantage of education that is not under the monopolistic control of the government would be the consumer's greater ability to influence what is offered. Experience reveals that many parents are not satisfied with the conditions of study under the public school education system: crowded classrooms that prevent efficient learning and help spread disease; the heat in summer and the cold in winter for lack of air conditioning; the lack of the necessary technologically advanced equipment.

Whoever bestows "free" education determines the methods used and the conditions of study. On the other hand, when education is private and dependent upon profit, the consumers can influence the educational methods used, just as they can influence the supply of all other services and goods on the market.

Education that is not in the monopolistic purview of the government would also have considerable advantage from the standpoint of changing the status of the woman, who would be able to exert greater influence upon educational content. Government-controlled public education is an obstacle to women's advancement, because those who determine policy are liable to construct curricula that women would not choose willingly.

As in all other spheres, this highly depends on how women perceive the situation and how ready they are to act accordingly: the benefit of girls demands that parents prepare them for the kind of life that awaits them in a free state from an early age – responsibility and effort. Until now, parents and other agents of socialization have prepared only the boys for work, advancement, and achievement.

In a free state, the woman would be obliged to take responsibility for her own livelihood; therefore, the parents would need to raise their daughters first and foremost to be economically independent, by providing them with an education and serious professional training. Today, those whose education did not go beyond high school studies already have difficulty finding employment. More than half the additional jobs offered today demand a post-high school education.[22] In order to prepare girls properly for living today, parents must provide them with an education which meets the needs of their development, happiness, and self-esteem. Government education is liable to convey stereotypes that could slant the development of boys and girls in particular directions, and via the educational material, instill in girls the perception that they are inferior. When education is nationalized, parents and young girls cannot opt for an education that is not sexist in orientation, since they are not offered alternatives. This is not the case in a free state where parents pay directly for education and can choose between different and varied content, teaching methods, and educational approaches, including, among other things, how they relate to boys and girls. If the parents wish to prepare their daughters for a life of economic independence, development, and self-esteem, they would be able to do so; they could send their daughters to pre-schools and schools in which girls are treated with respect and as equals and refrain from sending them to educational institutions that degrade women. By choosing to purchase or not to purchase a particular educational service, these parents would determine which educational approaches would thrive and which would disappear. Schools that provide the desired education would be in greater demand and thus generate larger profits, whereas other schools would lose money and be forced to close down if they did not change their methods. Economic sanctions would impel business owners to correct a discriminatory situation if they wanted to survive economically.

In a free economy, representing the woman in an insulting manner would do economic damage, not only to owners of kindergartens and schools but also to writers, moviemakers, radio and television network owners, and newspaper publishers whose profits would depend upon women as consumers.

In a free state, discrimination against women would not be a rational option. But a rational approach could not be dictated by law; the right of the employer or producer to discriminate against women would also be protected. It would be possible to fight such discrimination only by means of economic boycott or social disapprobation.

Even if we assume that the desired change in how business owners relate to women did not occur and they remained adamant in their discriminatory policies and did not employ women or cooperate with women in their work, even then, women would not be stymied. Women would always have the opportunity of dealing with more enlightened men or with other women, as men have been accustomed to doing for thousands of years, when they conducted their affairs without the participation of women. If women were discriminated against, they would be able to establish schools and universities on their own, set up their own businesses, and as a last resort, to cooperate only with members of their own sex: to establish orchestras consisting only of women, hospitals whose staffs were entirely female, etc.

Although it is commonly agreed that the standard of living is higher in a free state, there are those who argue that such a system might hurt the lower strata of society, those who are not able to work for their livelihood. The solution for such people would be provided by insurance they would have acquired earlier. For example, the woman could insure herself prior to childbirth in the event that the child would be abnormal (although technological progress would make possible a substantial decrease of defective births). Insurance could also constitute a solution for other problems such as unemployment, loss of the ability to work either temporarily or permanently, performance of an expensive operation, prolonged treatment in the case of illness – problems which lead women to favor a welfare state. Insurance would enable the woman to survive difficult times, without her transferring the burden of her existence to others. Thus, it is not necessary for women to prefer a welfare state, which controls almost all areas of their lives and denies them a life of well-being only in order to "ensure" assistance in time of need (assistance that is by no means guaranteed).

The basic requirement of life in a free state is the woman's readiness to accept responsibility for her life. To this demand, one woman may react positively – rejoice in the freedom of action which is now possible for her, whereas another might see it as threatening and difficult and would want to transfer responsibility for her livelihood to others.

A woman who was uncertain as to her ability to take care of herself and who would want to live under an organized form of life in accordance with the principle of distribution according to need would be able, in a free state, to join a voluntary cooperative framework, like the *kibbutz* in Israel, or she could establish such a framework herself. A woman could also remain "conservative" if she so desired. It may be presumed that at least in the near future there would be some men who are still interested in marrying a woman who would be dependent upon them and would live mostly for them despite the damage this entails for the woman and even for the man. We have already been there, but we have not yet been in a completely free state, in which the ideal of a life of sacrifice has not been imposed on women, in which one person does not rule another, and one sex is not superior to the other.

Considering the opportunities the free state offers for its realization, it would seem that feminism, as currently practiced, is only at the beginning of its journey.

Notes

Introduction

1. Betty Friedan, "It Changed My Life," W.W. Norton & Co., New York and London, 1985, pp. 153, 245-246, 316.

    Betty Friedan, *The Feminine Mystique*, Dell Publishing Co. Inc., New York, 1974, pp. 164-167.

2. Shere Hite, *Women and Love: A Cultural Revolution in Progress*, New York, St. Martin's Press, 1989, pp. 387-388.

3. Sylvia Ann Hewlett, *A Lesser Life, The Myth of Women's Liberation in America*, William Morrow and Company, New York, 1986, p. 402.

4. Hite, *Women and Love*, pp. 396-397.

    Shere Hite, *The Hite Report on Male Sexuality*, Macdonald & Co. Ltd., London, 1990, p. 312.

5. Hewlett, A Lesser Life, pp. 402-403.

6. Friedan, "It Changed My Life," pp. 138-139, 250, 375.

    Friedan, *The Feminine Mystique*, pp. 365-366.

7. Friedan, "It Changed My Life," pp. xxii, 245-246, 258.

    Friedan, *The Feminine Mystique*, p. 374.

8. Friedan, "It Changed My Life," p. 388.

9. Toni Grant, *Being A Woman: Fulfilling Your Femininity and Finding Love*, Random House, New York, 1988.

   Hite, *Women and Love*, pp. 403-404.

10. Morwenna Griffiths and Margaret Whitford, Eds., *Feminist Perspectives*, Macmillan Press Ltd., London, 1988, p. 34.

11. Dale Spender, Ed., *Men's Studies Modified*, Pergamon Press, Great Britain, 1987, p. 48.

12. Ellen Kennedy and Susan Mendus, Eds., *Women in Western Political Philosophy*, Wheatsheaf Books, Great Britain, 1987, p. 175.

13. Simone de Beauvoir, *The Second Sex*, Bantam Books, New York, 1961, pp. 639-640.

14. Mary Roth Walsh, Ed., *The Psychology of Women*, Yale University Press, New Haven and London, 1987, pp. 249, 251, 278-320.

   Carol Gilligan, *In A Different Voice: Psychological Theory and Women's Development*, Harvard University Press, Cambridge, 1982.

   Adrienne Rich, *Of Woman Born: Motherhood as Experience and Institution*, W.W. Norton & Co., New York, 1976, p. 46.

15. Hewlett, *A Lesser Life*.

   Rich, *Of Woman Born*, Tenth Anniversary Edition, W.W. Norton & Co., New York, 1986, chapter added ten years later.

16. Rich, *ibid*.

   Hewlett, *A Lesser Life*, pp. 76-77, 373-374, 377-379.

17. Hewlett, *ibid*, pp. 27-28, 147, 169.

   Barbara Ehrenreich and Deirdre English, *For Her Own Good*, Pluto Press, London, 1988, pp. 321-324.

18. Kennedy and Mendus, *Women in Western Political Philosophy*, pp. 15-18.

    John Stuart Mill, *On Liberty*, Basil Blackwell, Oxford, 1946.

    John Stuart Mill and Harriet Taylor Mill, *Essays on Sex Equality*, University of Chicago Press, Chicago, 1970.

19. Peter Schwartz, *The Battle for Laissez-Faire Capitalism*, New York, 1983.

    Rose Wilder Lane, *The Discovery of Freedom*, Arno Press of the New York Times, New York, 1972.

The Nature of Woman
The Determinist View of Feminine Attributes

1. Aristotle, *The Politics*, Penguin Books, England, 1973.

    Jean-Jacques Rousseau, *Emile*, Dent, London, 1974.

    Immanuel Kant, *The Metaphysical Elements of Justice*, Bobbs-Merrill, Indianapolis, 1965.

    Immanuel Kant, *Anthropology from a Pragmatic Point of View*, Martinus Nijhoff, The Hague, 1974.

    G.F.W. Hegel, *The Philosophy of Right*, Oxford University Press, Oxford, 1967.

    G.F.W. Hegel, *The Phenomenology of Spirit*, Macdonald & Co. Ltd., London, 1990.

2. Cynthia Fuchs Epstein, Deceptive Distinctions, Yale University Press, New Haven and London & Russell Sage Foundation, New York, 1988, pp. 3-4.

    Walsh, *The Psychology of Women*, p. 99.

3. de Beauvoir, The Second Sex, p. 237.

4. Elisabeth Badinter, *The Myth of Motherhood: A Historical*

View of the Maternal Instinct, Souvenir Press (E & A) Ltd., London, 1981, pp. 278-298.

5. Ha-aretz, 7.3.1991 (Hebrew).

6. Walsh, *The Psychology of Women*, pp. 249, 279-319.

Women by Nature Are Not Creative and Do Not Excel in Any Sphere

1. Kennedy and Mendus, *Women in Western Political Philosophy*, pp. 86-88.

   Badinter, *The Myth of Motherhood*, pp. 208-230.

2. Susan Griffin, *Woman and Nature*, The Women's Press, Great Britain, 1978, pp. 20-26.

   Kennedy and Mendus, *Women in Western Political Philosophy*, pp. 86-88, 140-156.

3. Badinter, The Myth of Motherhood, pp. 208-230.

4. de Beauvoir, The Second Sex, p. 131.

5. Badinter, The Myth of Motherhood, pp. 208-230.

6. Amnon Levy, *The Ultra-Orthodox*, Keter, Jerusalem, 1990 (Hebrew).

7. *ibid.*

   Moses Maimonides, *Mishneh Torah*, Mozna'im, 1986.

   —, *Guide of the Perplexed*, University of Chicago Press, Chicago, 1963.

8. Badinter, *The Myth of Motherhood*, pp. 10-15.

9. Friedan, *The Feminine Mystique*, pp. 79-80.

10. Rita Freedman, *Beauty Bound*, Columbus Books, London, 1988, pp. 93-94.

11. Friedan, "It Changed My Life," p. 339.

12. Epstein, *Deceptive Distinctions*, pp. 235-236.

13. Virginia Woolf, *A Room of One's Own*, Harcourt Brace Janovich, New York, 1991 [1929].

    de Beauvoir, *The Second Sex*, pp. 98-99, 312-313, 657-660, 670.

    Marcia Westkott, *The Feminist Legacy of Karen Horney*, Yale University Press,

    New Haven and London, 1986, pp. 83-85, 96, 120-121.

14. de Beauvoir, *The Second Sex*, pp. 433, 575.

15. Epstein, *Deceptive Distinctions*, pp. 54, 133, 205.

16. de Beauvoir, *The Second Sex*, pp. 438, 533-534, 575, 675.

    Kennedy and Mendus, *Women in Western Political Philosophy*, p. 113.

17. Epstein, *Deceptive Distinctions*, pp. 54, 133.

18. *ibid*, pp. 120-122.

19. B.B.C. *International*, 8.5.1991.

20. Friedan, *The Feminine Mystique*, pp. 76-77.

21. Epstein, *Deceptive Distinctions*, pp. 122-125.

22. Hite, *Women and Love*, p. 329.

23. Kennedy, *Women in Western Political Philosophy*, pp. 113, 164.

    Friedan, *The Feminine Mystique*, pp. 81-86.

24. de Beauvoir, *The Second Sex*, p. 89.

25. Badinter, *The Myth of Motherhood*, pp. 82-84, 86-88, 140-141.

26. Cited in Hewlett, *A Lesser Life*, p. 85.

27. Epstein, *Deceptive Distinctions*, pp. 120-122, 125.

28. de Beauvoir, *The Second Sex*, pp. 123, 591.

29. Alvin Toffler, *The Third Wave*, William Morrow & Co., New York, 1980, p. 66.

30. de Beauvoir, *The Second Sex*, pp. 657-660.

31. Friedan, *The Feminine Mystique*, pp. 60-61, 174-176.

   Friedan, "It Changed My Life," pp. 62-63.

32. Rich, *Of Woman Born*, 1976, p. 205.

33. Epstein, *Deceptive Distinctions*, p. 140.

34. Hite, *Women and Love*, pp. 475-477.

   Marcia Westkott, *The Feminist Legacy of Karen Horney*, pp. 120-121.

35. Hite, *The Hite Report on Male Sexuality*, pp. 62, 292.

36. Kathy Keeton, *Woman of Tomorrow*, St. Martin's Press, New York, 1985, pp. 309-311.

   Marcia Westkott, *The Feminist Legacy of Karen Horney*, pp. 120-121.

   Freedman, *Beauty Bound*, pp. 92-93, 115-116, 225.

37. Friedan, *The Feminine Mystique*, pp. 140-162, 164-176.

38. de Beauvoir, *The Second Sex*, pp. 337, 657-660.

   Friedan, *The Feminine Mystique*, pp. 67, 142-143, 147.

39. de Beauvoir, *The Second Sex*, p. 126.

40. Friedan, *The Feminine Mystique*, pp. 140-162.

   Keeton, *Woman of Tomorrow*, pp. 309-311.

41. Freedman, *Beauty Bound*, p. 25.

42. Friedan, *The Feminine Mystique*, pp. 53-54.

43. Badinter, *The Myth of Motherhood*, pp. 230-231.

44. *ibid*.

45. Friedan, *The Feminine Mystique*, pp. 141-142.

46. de Beauvoir, *The Second Sex*, pp. 313-314, 657-660.

47. Walsh, *The Psychology of Women*, p. 183.

48. Badinter, *The Myth of Motherhood*, p. 289.

49. *ibid*, pp. 244-245, 263-298.

   Hewlett, *A Lesser Life*, pp. 250, 257, 281-282, 327.

   Rich, *Of Woman Born*, 1976, pp. 17-18.

   Friedan, *The Feminine Mystique*, pp. 96-100.

   Walsh, *The Psychology of Women*, p. 76.

   Sigmund Freud, *New Introductory Lectures in Psychoanalysis*, Allen & Unwin, London, 1971.

   Sigmund Freud, *The Standard Edition of the Complete Psychological Works of Sigmund Freud*, Hagarth Press, London, Vol. 7, 1905; Vol. 18, 1922; Vol. 19, 1925.

50. Hite, *Women and Love*, pp. 690-693.

51. Badinter, *The Myth of Motherhood*, pp. 208-230.

   Friedan, *The Feminine Mystique*, pp. 37-38.

52. Badinter, *The Myth of Motherhood*.

53. *Hadashot*, 6.3.91 (Hebrew).

54. Epstein, *Deceptive Distinctions*, p. 148.

55. Freedman, *Beauty Bound*, p. 104.

56. de Beauvoir, *The Second Sex*, pp. 125-126, 657-660.

57. *ibid*, pp. 433-438, 575, 650.

   Kennedy, *Women in Western Political Philosophy*, p. 113.

58. Epstein, *Deceptive Distinctions*, p. 235.

59. *Davar Ha-shavua*, 12.22.1989 (Hebrew).

60. Keeton, *Woman of Tomorrow*, p. 77.

61. Freedman, *Beauty Bound*, pp. 94, 104.

62. Epstein, *Deceptive Distinctions*, pp. 66-68.

   Rich, *Of Woman Born*, 1976, p. 72.

63. Badinter, *The Myth of Motherhood*, pp. 278-298.

    Epstein, *Deceptive Distinctions*, pp. 85-87.

    Keeton, *Woman of Tomorrow*, pp. 42-43.

    Friedan, *The Feminine Mystique*, pp. 96-100.

    Walsh, *The Psychology of Women*, pp. 237-238.

    Griffiths and Whitford, *Feminist Perspectives*, p. 94.

    de Beauvoir, *The Second Sex*, pp. 37, 44-47, 261, 675, 684.

Women Live For Others

1. Walsh, *The Psychology of Women*, p. 211.

    Hite, *The Hite Report on Male Sexuality*, p. 64.

2. Epstein, *Deceptive Distinctions*, p. 59.

    Gilligan, *In a Different Voice*.

    Walsh, *The Psychology of Women*, pp. 278-319.

3. *ibid*, pp. 323-328.

4. Epstein, *Deceptive Distinctions*, pp. 82-83.

5. *ibid*, pp. 82-83.

6. Friedan, "It Changed My Life," pp. 79, 133.

7. Hite, *Women and Love*, pp. 103-107, 117-119, 131-132, 316, 622-623.

    Rich, *Of Woman Born*, 1976, pp. 172-173.

    Westkott, *The Feminist Legacy of Karen Horney*, pp. 146, 158-159.

    Walsh, *The Psychology of Women*, pp. 91-95.

    Freedman, *Beauty Bound*, pp. 103, 114-115.

8. Hite, *The Hite Report on Male Sexuality*, p. 787.

9. *ibid*, p. 730, 942.

10. Hite, *Women and Love*, pp. 260-261.

11. *ibid*, pp. 281-282, 443-444.

12. *ibid*, pp. 127, 260-261, 404-405, 590n.

13. Badinter, *The Myth of Motherhood*, pp. 263-298.

    Hewlett, *A Lesser Life*, p. 250.

    Friedan, *The Feminine Mystique*, pp. 96-100.

    Walsh, *The Psychology of Women*, p. 76.

14. *ibid*, pp. 86-87, 91-95.

15. Badinter, *The Myth of Motherhood*.

Women Are Motivated By Emotions

1. Hite, *Women and Love*, p. 650.

2. *ibid*, p. 659-662.

3. Kennedy and Mendus, *Women in Western Political Philosophy*, pp. 155-158.

4. Epstein, *Deceptive Distinctions*, pp. 232-234.

   Griffiths and Whitford, *Feminist Perspectives*, pp. 17, 131-136.

   Marian Lowe and Ruth Hubbard, *Woman's Nature*, Pergamon Press, Great Britain, 1986, pp. 13-14.

5. Griffiths and Whitford, *Feminist Perspectives*, pp. 131-136.

Additional Determinist Arguments

1. Hite, *Women and Love*, pp. 628-631.

   Lowe and Hubbard, *Woman's Nature*, p. 89.

2. Epstein, *Deceptive Distinctions*, p. 59.

3. Lowe and Hubbard, *Woman's Nature*, p. 92.

4. Hite, *Women and Love*, p. 84.

5. Nancy Friday, *Jealousy*, Perigord Press, William Morrow and Company Inc., New York, 1985, p. 368.

6. Keeton, Woman of Tomorrow, p. 47.

7. Epstein, *Deceptive Distinctions*, pp. 201-203.

8. Ehrenreich and English, *For Her Own Good*, p. 124.

9. Walsh, *The Psychology of Women*, pp. 166, 200.

10. Rosalind Miles, *The Women's History of the World*, Paladin, Gradton Books, London, 1990, p. 226.

11. Epstein, *Deceptive Distinctions*, pp. 219-220.

12. de Beauvoir, *The Second Sex*, p. 572.

13. Badinter, *The Myth of Motherhood*, pp. 63-64.

14. Epstein, *Deceptive Distinctions*, pp. 168-169.
    Hadashot, 6.7.1991 (Hebrew).

15. Hite, *Women and Love*, p. 232.

16. de Beauvoir, *The Second Sex*, pp. 424-425.

17. Epstein, *Deceptive Distinctions*, pp. 56-57.

18. Freedman, *Beauty Bound*, p. 187.

19. Friday, *Jealousy*, p. 372.

20. Hite, *The Hite Report on Male Sexuality*, pp. 476-477, 757.

21. *ibid*, pp. 616, 649, 702-703, 707, 1060.
    Hite, *Women and Love*, pp. 77-78, 143-144, 146-147, 173-174, 449-450.

What Remains of the Argument That There Are Innate Differences Between the Sexes?

1. Epstein, *Deceptive Distinctions*, pp. 18-19, 21.

Keeton, *Woman of Tomorrow*, pp. 32-34, 64-76.

2. Lowe and Hubbard, *Woman's Nature*, p. 125.

3. Epstein, *Deceptive Distinctions*, pp. 67-70.

    Margaret Mead, *Sex and Temperament in Three Primitive Societies*, William Morrow, New York, 1935.

4. Friedan, *The Feminine Mystique*, pp. 127-130, 305-309.

5. Epstein, *Deceptive Distinctions*, pp. 59, 231.

6. Badinter, *The Myth of Motherhood*, p. 328.

7. Epstein, *Deceptive Distinctions*, pp. 18-19.

    Keeton, *Woman of Tomorrow*, pp. 32-34, 64, 67.

8. Hite, *Women and Love*, p. 663n.

9. Epstein, *Deceptive Distinctions*, pp. 44-45, 59, 81, 219-220.

10. Ehrenreich and English, *For Her Own Good*, pp. 59, 244-248.

11. Epstein, *Deceptive Distinctions*, pp. 231-234.

12. Walsh, *The Psychology of Women*, pp. 237-238.

13. Epstein, *Deceptive Distinctions*, pp. 139-140, 199-202.

14. *ibid*, pp. 89-90, 96.

15. Hite, *Women and Love*, p. 133n.

16. Epstein, *Deceptive Distinctions*, pp. 89-90, 96.

17. Westkott, *The Feminist Legacy of Karen Horney*, pp. 200-201.

18. Keeton, *Woman of Tomorrow*, pp. 283-284.

19. *ibid*, pp. iv, xviii, 77-79.

de Beauvoir, *The Second Sex*, p. 48.

20. Walsh, *The Psychology of Women*, pp. 222-223.

21. Westkott, *The Feminist Legacy of Karen Horney*, pp. 200-201.

Women's Suffering in Their Traditional Feminine Role

1. Friedan, *The Feminine Mystique*, pp. 38-39, 112-113, 351.

    Ehrenreich and English, *For Her Own Good*, pp. 206, 221, 269-270.

    Helene Deutsch, *The Psychology of Women, A Psychoanalytical Interpretation*,

    Grune and Straton, New York, 1944, Vol.1, pp. 224, 251.

2. Charles Murray, *In Pursuit of Happiness and Good Government*,

    Simon and Schuster, New York, 1988, pp. 52-53, 76.

    Abraham H. Maslow, *Motivation and Personality*, 3rd edition, Harper and Row, New York, 1987.

3. Joseph Raz, *The Morality of Freedom*, Clarendon Press, Oxford, 1988, pp. 306-307.

4. Freedman, *Beauty Bound*, pp. 28-30.

    Walsh, *The Psychology of Women*, p. 99.

    Friedan, *The Feminine Mystique*, pp. 299, 301, 303-306.

5. *ibid*, p. 11-13.

6. Freedman, *Beauty Bound*, pp. 80-81.

    Friday, *Jealousy*, p. 496.

7. Hite, *Women and Love*, p. 478.

8. Walsh, *The Psychology of Women*, pp. 110-111.

9. Friedan, *The Feminine Mystique*, pp. 16-17, 44, 226, 351, 367.

10. *ibid*, pp. 244-245.

11. Friedan, "It Changed My Life," pp. 64, 68-69.

12. Hewlett, *A Lesser Life*, pp. 323-324.

13. Friedan, "It Changed My Life," pp. 64, 68-69.

14. de Beauvoir, *The Second Sex*, pp. 425-428.

15. Hewlett, *A Lesser Life*, pp. 231-325.

    Mirra Komarovsky, *Woman in the Modern World*, Little Brown,Boston, 1953,

pp. 108-110, (cited in Hewlett, A Lesser Life, pp. 324-325).

16. Murray, *In Pursuit of Happiness and Good Government*, pp. 146-147.

17. Friedan, *The Feminine Mystique*, pp. 172, 225-226, 367.

18. Freedman, *Beauty Bound*, pp. 200-207.

19. *ibid*, pp. 35, 105, 195, 200-207.

20. Hite, *Women and Love*, pp. 625-626.

21. Hewlett, *A Lesser Life*, pp. 12-13.

    Allan Bloom, *The Closing of the American Mind: How Higher Education Has Failed Democracy and Impoverished the Souls of Today's Students*, Simon & Schuster, New York, 1987, pp. 126-127.

22. Hite, *Women and Love*, pp. 122-123, 125-126, 380, 615-621, 671-672, 674.

23. Hewlett, *A Lesser Life*, p. 66.

24. *Globes*, 4.27.1990 (Hebrew).

25. Friedan, *The Feminine Mystique*, pp. 249, 310-320.

26. Keeton, *Woman of Tomorrow*, pp. 85-86, 109-114.

Woman and the Other

Women's Traditional Role is of Benefit to Men

1. Miles, *The Women's History of the World*, p. 224.

2. de Beauvoir, *The Second Sex*, pp. 685-689.

3. Hite, *The Hite Report on Male Sexuality*, p. 923.

4. Friedan, *The Feminine Mystique*, p. 42.

5. Badinter, *The Myth of Motherhood*, pp. 322-325.

6. Hite, *The Hite Report on Male Sexuality*, pp. 11, 314.

7. *ibid*, p. 305.

8. *ibid*, pp. 282-283, 761.

9. Friedan, *The Feminine Mystique*, pp. 341-342.

10. Elaine Morgan, *The Descent of Woman*, Souvenir Press, London, 1985, p. 237.

11. de Beauvoir, *The Second Sex*, p. 447.

12. Hite, *The Hite Report on Male Sexuality*, pp. 283, 316, 942.

13. *ibid*, pp. 65, 67, 283, 294-295, 762, 795.

    Hite, *Women and Love*, pp. 104-105, 117-119.

14. Friedan, *The Feminine Mystique*, pp. 89, 363-364.

    Kennedy and Mendus, *Women in Western Political Philosophy*, p. 120.

15. Hite, *The Hite Report on Male Sexuality*, p. 316.

16. *ibid*, p. 318.

Women's Traditional Role Benefits the Children

1. Epstein, *Deceptive Distinctions*, pp. 197-198.

    Keeton, *Woman of Tomorrow*, p. 204.

2. *ibid*, pp. 208-212.

    Friedan, *The Feminine Mystique*, pp. 180-187.

3. Friday, *Jealousy*, pp. 86-87.

Rich, *Of Woman Born*, 1976, pp. 167-168.

4. Hite, *The Hite Report on Male Sexuality*, p. 117.

5. *ibid*, p. 118.

6. Epstein, *Deceptive Distinctions*, pp. 197-198.

7. Ehrenreich and English, *For Her Own Good*, p. 229.

8. de Beauvoir, *The Second Sex*, pp. 484-486, 492.

9. *ibid*, pp. 494-495.

10. *ibid*, pp. 484-486, 494-495.

    Ehrenreich and English, *For Her Own Good*, pp. 184-185.

11. Friedan, *The Feminine Mystique*, pp. 24, 181, 184.

12. *ibid*, pp. 187-190.

13. Keeton, *Woman of Tomorrow*, pp. 206-207.

14. Friedan, *The Feminine Mystique*, pp. 24, 181, 184.

15. Hewlett, *A Lesser Life*, p. 344.

16. Keeton, *Woman of Tomorrow*, pp. 208-212.

17. Friday, *Jealousy*, pp. 72-73, 317-320.

18. Hite, *The Hite Report on Male Sexuality*, p. 115.

19. Hite, *Women and Love*, pp. 412-413.

The Contribution of Feminism

1. Bernard Williams, *Problems of the Self*, Cambridge University Press, Cambridge, 1973, pp. 250-251.

    Raz, *The Morality of Freedom*, pp. 32, 213, 312.

2. Friedan, *The Feminine Mystique*, pp. 10, 54-56, 64-65, 71-72, 322-324.

    Rich, *Of Woman Born*, 1976, p. 20.

3. Westkott, *The Feminist Legacy of Karen Horney*, pp. 200-201.

The Political Solution | The Communist State

1. Lowe and Hubbard, *Women's Nature*, p. 91.

    Rich, *Of Woman Born*, 1976, pp. 80-82.

    Karl Marx and Friedrich Engels, *The Communist Manifesto*, Gateway Editions Inc., Henry Regnery Company, Chicago, 1954.

    Karl Marx, *Early Writings*, tr. and ed. by T.B. Bootomore, London: Watts & Co., 1963.

    K. Marx and F. Engels, *Selected Works*, Vols. I & II, Foreign Languages Publishing House, Moscow, 1950.

2. Friedan, *The Feminine Mystique*, pp. 10, 54-56, 64-65, 71-72, 322-324.

    Rich, *Of Woman Born*, 1976, pp. 20, 69, 80-82.

    Epstein, *Deceptive Distinctions*, pp. 152-153.

    Friedan, "It Changed My Life," p. 102.

3. *ibid*, pp. 102, 364.

4. Rich, *Of Woman Born*, 1976, pp. 80-82.

5. Epstein, *Deceptive Distinctions*, pp. 152-153.

6. Hedrick Smith, *The Russians*, Times Books, New York, 1983, pp. 180-181.

7. Rich, *Of Woman Born*, 1976, pp. 227-228.

8. de Beauvoir, *The Second Sex*, pp. 117-118.

9. Epstein, *Deceptive Distinctions*, pp. 52-54, 126.

    Rich, *Of Woman Born*, 1976, pp. 30-31.

10. Friedan, "It Changed My Life," p. 364.

11. Miles, *The Women's History of the World*, p. 280.

12. Friedan, "It Changed My Life," p. 364.

13. Smith, *The Russians*, pp. 166-440.

The Welfare State

1. Karl Mannheim, *Freedom, Power, and Democratic Planning*, Routledge & Kegan Paul Ltd., London, 1951, pp. 29, 177.

2. Thomas Sowell, *Knowledge and Decisions*, Basic Books Inc., New York, 1980, pp. 119-120.

3. Robert Nozick, *Anarchy*, State and Utopia, Basic Books Inc., New York, 1974, pp. 169-172.

4. Herbert Marcuse, *One-Dimensional Man*: Studies in the Ideology of Advanced Industrial Society, Beacon Press, Boston, 1964.

   Rich, *Of Woman Born*, 1976.

5. Milton Friedman, *Capitalism and Freedom*, The University of Chicago Press, Chicago, 1962, p. 200.

6. *Ha-aretz*, 3.6.1990 (Hebrew).

7. Murray, *In Pursuit of Happiness and Good Government*, pp. 264-274; this dialogue follows Murray's example.

8. Sowell, *Knowledge and Decisions*, p. 359.

9. Thomas Sowell, *Ethnic America*, Basic Books, New York, 1981.

10. Hewlett, *A Lesser Life*, pp. 237-248.

11. *Maariv*, 5.22.1991 (Hebrew).

12. Freedman, *Beauty Bound*, pp. 121-122.

13. Epstein, *Deceptive Distinctions*, p. 57.

14. Hewlett, *A Lesser Life*, pp. 237-248.

15. *ibid*, pp. 278-279.

16. Bernard Dixon, *What Is Science For?* Collins, London, 1973.

17. Lowe and Hubbard, *Woman's Nature*, p. 50.

18. *Niv Hagimlai*, Tel Aviv, March 1990, p. 88 (Hebrew).

19. *Ha-aretz*, 9.15.1983 (Hebrew).

20. Friedan, "It Changed My Life," pp. 246-247.

21. Rich, *Of Woman Born*, 1976, p. 64.

Utopia – The Free State

1. Rich, *Of Woman Born*, 1976, p. 226.

2. Miles, *The Women's History of the World*, pp. 103-123, 302.

    Scilla McLean, *Minority Rights Group Report*, No. 47, December 1980.

    Ha-aretz, 7.19.1991 (Hebrew).

3. Additional information on the structure of the free state and on

    its dynamic can be found in: Gizi Rapaport, *Freedom or Equality?*,

    University Press of America, 2012.

4. Rich, *Of Woman Born*, 1976, p. 30.

    Lee Sanders Comer, *Functions of the Family Under Capitalism*, pamphlet reprinted by the New York Radical Feminists, 1974.

5. Sowell, *Knowledge and Decisions*, pp. 115-118, 151, 244.

    Ayn Rand, *Capitalism: The Unknown Ideal*, A Signet Book, The New American Library, 1967, pp. 46-47.

6. Keeton, *Woman of Tomorrow*, pp. 303-304.

7. Hewlett, *A Lesser Life*, pp. 233-235.

8. Friedan, *The Feminine Mystique*, pp. 322-324.

9. Hewlett, *A Lesser Life*, pp. 235-236.

10. Ehrenreich and English, *For Her Own Good*, pp. 318-319.

11. *Yediot Ahronot*, 12.8.1989 (Hebrew).

    Michael Novak, *The American Vision*, American Enterprise Institute, Washington, D.C., 1978.

12. Badinter, *The Myth of Motherhood*, p. 314.

13. Hewlett, *A Lesser Life*, pp. 318-321.

14. *ibid*, p. 127.

15. *Yediot Ahronot*, 3.21.1990 (Hebrew).

16. Hewlett, *A Lesser Life*, pp. 82-85.

Friedan, "It Changed My Life," p. 12.

17. *Ha-aretz*, 5.2.1991 (Hebrew).

18. Friedan, *The Feminine Mystique*, pp. 337-338.

19. *ibid*, pp. 227-234, 241-242.

20. Ludwig von Mises, *Bureaucracy*, Yale University Press, New Haven, Connecticut and London, 1944, pp. 13-14.

    Ludwig von Mises, *Planning for Freedom*, Second Edition, Libertarian Press, South Holland, Illinois, 1961.

    Henri Lepage, *Tomorrow, Capitalism*, Open Court Publishing Company, La Salle, Illinois, 1982, pp. 34-35.

21. George Reisman, *The Government Against the Economy*, Caroline House Publishers Inc., New York, 1979.

    George Reisman, *Capitalism: The Cure For Racism*, pamphlet, 1991.

22. Fortune, 16.3.1990.

Selected Bibliography

Badinter, Elisabeth. *The Myth of Motherhood: An Historical View of the Maternal Instinct.* London: Souvenir Press (E & A) Ltd., 1981.

Beauvoir, Simone de. *The Second Sex,* New York: Bantam Books, 1961.

Ehrenreich, Barbara, and Deirdre English. London: *For Her Own Good,* Pluto Press, 1988.

Epstein, Cynthia Fuchs. *Deceptive Distinctions: Sex, Gender and the Social Order.* New Haven and London: Russell Sage Foundation, 1988.

Freedman, Rita. *Beauty Bound.* London: Columbus Books, 1988.

Friedan, Betty. *The Feminine Mystique.* New York: Dell Publishing Co. Inc., 1974.

——. "It Changed My Life." London: W.W. Norton & Co. New York, 1985.

Gilligan, Carol. *In a Different Voice: Psychological Theory and Women's Development.* Cambridge: Harvard University Press, 1982.

Griffin, Susan. *Woman and Nature.* London: The Women's Press, 1978.

Griffiths, Morwenna, and Margaret Whitford, Eds. *Feminist Perspectives*. London: Macmillan Press Ltd., 1988.

Hewlett, Sylvia Ann. *A Lesser Life: The Myth of Women's Liberation in America*. New York: William Morrow and Company, 1986.

Hite, Shere. *The Hite Report on Male Sexuality*. London: Macdonald & Co. Ltd., 1990.

——. *Women and Love: A Cultural Revolution in Progress*. New York: St. Martin's Press, 1989.

Keeton, Kathy. *Woman of Tomorrow*. New York: St. Martin's Press, 1985.

Kennedy, Ellen, and Susan Mendus, Eds. *Women in Western Political Philosophy*. London: Wheatsheaf Books, 1987.

Lowe, Marian, and Ruth Hubbard, Eds. London: *Woman's Nature*, Pergamon Press, 1986.

Miles, Rosalind. London: *The Women's History of the World*, Paladin, 1990.

Mill, John Stuart, and Harriet Taylor Mill. *Essays on Sex Equality*. Chicago: University of Chicago Press, 1970.

Morgan, Elaine. *The Descent of Woman*. London: Souvenir Press, 1985.

Rapaport, Gizi. *Freedom or Equality?* University Press of America, 2012.

Rich, Adrienne. *Of Woman Born: Motherhood as Experience and Institution*. New York: W.W. Norton & Co., 1976. Also, Tenth Anniversary Edition, 1986.

Spender, Dale, Ed. *Men's Studies Modified.* London: Pergamon Press, 1987.

Walsh, Mary Roth, Ed. *The Psychology of Women.* New Haven and London: Yale University Press, 1987.

Westkott, Marcia. *The Feminist Legacy of Karen Horney.* New Haven and London: Yale University Press, 1986.

Woolf, Virginia. *A Room of One's Own.* Harcourt Brace Janovich, New York: 1991, [1929].

9 781974 659456